The Hope of Glory

To Know Jesus and Live Through Him

Doug Baker

TEACH Services, Inc.
PUBLISHING
www.TEACHServices.com • (800) 367-1844

World rights reserved. This book or any portion thereof may not be copied or reproduced in any form or manner whatever, except as provided by law, without the written permission of the publisher, except by a reviewer who may quote brief passages in a review.

The author assumes full responsibility for the accuracy of all facts and quotations as cited in this book. The opinions expressed in this book are the author's personal views and interpretations, and do not necessarily reflect those of the publisher.

This book is provided with the understanding that the publisher is not engaged in giving spiritual, legal, medical, or other professional advice. If authoritative advice is needed, the reader should seek the counsel of a competent professional.

Copyright © 2014 TEACH Services, Inc.
ISBN-13: 978-1-4796-0441-8 (Paperback)
ISBN-13: 978-1-4796-0442-5 (ePub)
ISBN-13: 978-1-4796-0443-2 (Mobi)
Library of Congress Control Number: 2015910311

All scripture quotations, unless otherwise indicated, are taken from the King James Version. Public domain.

Scripture quotations marked (NIV) are taken from the Holy Bible, New International Version®, NIV®. Copyright © 1973, 1978, 1984, 2011 by Biblica, Inc.™ Used by permission of Zondervan. All rights reserved worldwide

Here, where the Son of God tabernacled in humanity; where the King of glory lived and suffered and died,—here, when He shall make all things new, the tabernacle of God shall be with men, "and He shall dwell with them, and they shall be His people, and God Himself, shall be with them, and be their God." And through endless ages as the redeemed walk in the light of the Lord, they will praise Him for His unspeakable Gift, Immanuel, "God with us."

Ellen G. White, "Heaven's Unspeakable Gift,"
The Review and Herald, February 25, 1915

Preface

In his letter to the Ephesians, the apostle Paul wrote of his vision for the church of Christ, desiring that it should grow "unto the measure of the stature of the fulness of Christ."[1] It has been my experience that adolescents rarely have depth to their experience in Christ. Often it is the case that youth are baptized into an intellectual understanding of religion that lacks practice in the fundamentals of faith in Christ. Many times I have been asked about prayer, faith, and works by those who frankly did not know where to begin to seek Christ. It became clear to me that it would be a great help to my students if I were to lay out the foundation of a relationship with Christ, as well as the blueprint for personal growth in Christ. But perhaps the need for growth extends to all of us, regardless of age.

In both his letter to the Ephesians as well as his letter to the Hebrews, Paul expressed frustration over the deficient condition of those in his generation who were not rising to maturity in Christ. In the former he wrote that he longed for them to be "no more children, tossed to and fro, and carried about with every wind of doctrine."[2] In the latter he wrote, you "ought to be teachers, ... [but you] need that one teach you again which be the first principles of the oracles of God."[3] He went on to say that they are spiritual babies. Our generation experiences a similar "failure to launch."

Our culture is dominated by influences that lead away from Christ, and it seems that the church has largely fallen to their sway. Additionally, by in large as Christians, we have been feeding on a gospel that "is not bread" and does not satisfy the needs of the soul.[4] The concept

---

1–Ephesians 4:13
2–Ephesians 4:14
3–Hebrews 5:12
4–Isaiah 55:2

of sanctification is largely lost, and as a result, many lack a vibrant Christian life.

In Paul's letter to the Ephesians he prayed that they would comprehend the dimensions of God's great love for them and, as a result, be filled with all the fullness of God.[5] He expressed to the Romans that rather than being conformed to the worldly mold, they could be "transformed by the renewing" of their minds.[6] To the Philippians he described the experience as having the mind of Christ.[7]

This experience of entering into a unity of mind with Christ was the object of Jesus' prayer on the night of His betrayal. Jesus prayed that we might have the same oneness of mind that He had with His Father.[8] This is the essence of growing into the fullness of the stature of Christ: to think as He did, and to live as He did.

This kind of knowledge is distinguished from the superficial experience of knowing about Christ. Such an experience is depicted in the parable of the ten virgins. To the foolish virgins, He spoke the words, "I know you not."[9] The similarity of the ten virgins is remarkable. The only mark of distinction is the presence of the flask with oil. But there is a great meaning in this difference. Both the wise and the foolish had an intellectual experience symbolized by the lamp.[10] Both the wise and the foolish had purity in deportment symbolized by their virginity. But the foolish lacked the experience symbolized by the flask.

"[T]he Lord himself shall give you a sign; Behold, a virgin shall conceive, and bear a son, and shall call his name Immanuel."[11] Christ living within is the concept shown in the prophecy of Isaiah, as well as in its fulfillment in the indwelling Christ. The foolish virgins did not have the indwelling of the Holy Spirit, which was shown by the clay flask with the precious oil. This is a symbolic illustration of the concept, "Emmanuel, ... God with us."[12] Paul refers to us as "earthen vessels" filled with treasure.[13] The experience of Mary symbolizes the experience of the Christian of having Christ formed within.

In contrast to the superficial knowledge of the foolish virgins, Jesus' words in His prayer for us as well as His disciples were, "this is life eternal, that they might know thee the only true God, and Jesus Christ, whom thou hast sent."[14] This book was written so that one may develop a deep experiential knowledge of God.

Ellen G. White was a prolific writer. Inspired by the Holy Spirit, she penned messages of hope and instruction that are as relevant today as they were in the mid to late 1800s and early 1900s when they were first published. In compiling this book, I have taken the liberty of extracting quotes from Mrs. White's books and magazine articles and joining them together in short "articles" that delineate practical steps of knowing Jesus

---

5–Ephesians 3:14-19
6–Romans 12:2
7–Philippians 2:5
8–John 17:20-22
9–Matthew 25:1-12
10–Psalm 119:105

11–Isaiah 7:14
12–Matthew 1:23
13–2 Corinthians 4:7
14–John 17:3

and living for Him. I have also capitalized certain words that may have been lowercased in her original writings, such as Heaven and names relating to God, etc.

This experience of growing up into Christ is well described in the words of John the Baptist: "He must increase, but I must decrease."[15] This experience, which Paul termed the mystery of God dwelling within, is the hope of experiencing the glory of the divine character manifested through us. Such an experience is our hope of glory.[16]

My prayer is that, as you read, your spiritual walk will be strengthened.

Doug Baker

For a complete list of the articles and books that Mrs. White wrote and that are quoted in The Hope of Glory, *please see the bibliography at the back of the book.*

15–John 3:30
16–Colossians 1:27

Table of Contents

Introduction 8

Chapter 1—Commitment 9

Chapter 2—Rest in Christ 14

Chapter 3—Devotion 20

Chapter 4—The Word 24

Chapter 5—Prayer Life 29

Chapter 6—Faith, Prayer, and the Power of the Word 35

Chapter 7—A Holy Name 39

Chapter 8—If You Love Me 42

Chapter 9—The Water of Death 47

Chapter 10—The Will 52

Chapter 11—Forgiveness 60

Chapter 12—The Only Way 65

Chapter 13—Pray for One Another 74

Chapter 14—In His Name 80

Chapter 15—Judgment 85

Chapter 16—The Cleansing 97

Chapter 17—Emmanuel 107

Bibliography 113

Introduction

"Seek ye first the Kingdom of God, and His righteousness; and all these things shall be added unto you." Matthew 6:33. This is the first great object—the Kingdom of Heaven, the righteousness of Christ. Other objects to be attained should be secondary to these.

Satan will present the path of holiness as difficult while the paths of worldly pleasure are strewed with flowers. In false and flattering colors will the tempter array the world with its pleasures before you. Vanity is one of the strongest traits of our depraved natures, and he knows that he can appeal to it successfully. He will flatter you through his agents. You may receive praise which will gratify your vanity and foster in you pride and self-esteem, and you may think that with such advantages and attractions it really is a great pity for you to come out from the world and be separate, and become a Christian.... But consider that the pleasures of Earth will have an end, and that which you sow you must also reap. Are personal attractions, ability, or talents too valuable to devote to God, the Author of your being, He Who watches over you every moment? Are your qualifications too precious to devote to God?

The young urge that they need something to enliven and divert the mind. I saw that there is pleasure in industry, a satisfaction in pursuing a life of usefulness. Some still urge that they must have something ... to which the mind can turn for relief and refreshment amid cares and wearing labor. The Christian's hope is just what is needed. Religion will prove to the believer a comforter, a sure guide to the Fountain of true happiness. The young should study the Word of God and give themselves to meditation and prayer, and they will find that their spare moment cannot be better employed.

Young friends, you should take time to prove your own selves, whether you are in the love of God. Be diligent to make your calling and election sure.

Seek first the Kingdom of God and His righteousness. Make his first and last. Seek most earnestly to know Him Whom to know aright is life eternal. Christ and His righteousness is the salvation of the soul.[17]

17–*Maranatha*, p. 71.

Chapter 1
Commitment

Friend of Sinners

Christ is the Friend of sinners. When the scribes and the Pharisees accused Him of eating with publicans and sinners, Jesus said, "I come not to call the righteous, but sinners to repentance." [Luke 5:32.] If you feel yourself to be the greatest of sinners, then Christ is just what you need; for He is the greatest of Saviours. Lift up your head, and look away from yourself, away from the poisoned wound of the serpent, to the Lamb of God, Who taketh away the sins of the world. What will all your groaning and the torturing of your soul avail? You may entertain thoughts that condemn you, but in them there is no salvation. Put away your thoughts, and receive the thoughts of God, through which your mind may be elevated, your soul purified and uplifted.... Why will you carry your burden of sin, when Christ has come to be your Burden Bearer? Roll your sins at the foot of the cross. Unload! unload! He takes away the sins of the world. "I, even I, am He that blotteth out thy transgressions for Mine Own sake, and will not remember thy sins." [Isaiah 43:25.][18]

A Client

Christ intercedes in behalf of those who have received Him. To them He gives power, by virtue of His Own merits, to become members of the Royal Family, children of the Heavenly King. And the Father demonstrates His infinite love for Christ, who paid our ransom with His blood, by receiving and welcoming Christ's friends as His friends. He is satisfied with the atonement made. He is glorified by the Incarnation, the life, death, and mediation of His Son. No sooner does the child of God approach the mercy seat than he becomes the client of the great Advocate. At his first utterance of penitence and appeal for pardon

---

18–*The Signs of the Times*, April 9, 1894.

Christ espouses his case and makes it His Own, presenting the supplication before the Father as His Own request.[19]

Ropes of Sand

Christ has said, "Without Me ye can do nothing." [John 15:5.] The resolutions you may make in your own finite strength, will be only as ropes of sand; but if you pray in sincerity, surrendering yourself, soul, body, and spirit, unto God, you put on the whole armor of God, and open the soul to the righteousness of Christ; and this alone,—Christ's imputed righteousness,—makes you able to stand against the wiles of the Devil. The work of every soul is to resist the enemy in the power and might of the Lord Jesus Christ, and the promise is that the Devil shall flee from us. But let all realize that they are in peril, and there is no assurance of safety except as they comply with the conditions of the text. The Lord says, "Draw nigh to God." [James 4:8.] How?—By secret, earnest examination of your own heart; by childlike, heartfelt, humble dependence upon God, making known your weakness to Jesus; and by confessing your sins. Thus you may draw nigh to God, and He will draw nigh to you.[20]

There are many who realize their helplessness, and who long for that spiritual life which will bring them into harmony with God; they are vainly striving to obtain this life. In despair they cry, "O wretched man that I am! Who shall deliver me from this body of death?" [Romans 7:24.] Let these desponding, despairing ones look up. The Saviour bids them arise in health and peace. Do not wait to feel that you are made whole. Believe His Word, and it will be fulfilled. Put your will on the side of Christ. Will to serve Him, and in acting upon His Word you will receive strength. Whatever may be the evil practice, the master passion, which through long indulgence binds you soul and body, Christ is able and longs to deliver…. He will set free the captive that is held by weakness and misfortune and the chains of sin.[21]

Many think that Christ is a long way off, and cannot hear when we cry to Him. But He is close to us, and He is acquainted with our weakness and our needs. He has borne our griefs and carried our sorrows. He understands our true condition.[22]

The relations between God and each soul are as distinct and full as though there were not another one for whom He gave His Beloved Son. The Lord is very pitiful and of tender mercy. His heart of love is touched by our sorrows, and even by our utterance of them…. There is … no sincere prayer [uttered] … of which our Heavenly Father is unobservant, or in which He does not take an immediate interest.[23]

Faith

The only faith that will benefit us is that which embraces Him as a personal Saviour; which appropriates His merits to ourselves…. [S]aving faith is a transaction, by which those who receive Christ join themselves in covenant rela-

---

19–*Testimonies for the Church*, vol. 6, pp. 363, 364.
20–*The Youth's Instructor*, February 8, 1894.
21–*The Signs of the Times*, January 20, 1904.
22–*Manuscript Releases*, vol. 3, p. 105.
23–*Pacific Health Journal*, December 1, 1901.

tion with God.[24] [M]any feel that they lack faith, and therefore they remain away from Christ. Let these souls, in their helpless unworthiness, cast themselves upon the mercy of their compassionate Saviour. Look not to self, but to Christ. He Who healed the sick and cast out demons when He walked among men is the same mighty Redeemer today. Faith comes by the Word of God. Then grasp His promise, "Him that cometh to Me I will in no wise cast out." John 6:37. Cast yourself at His feet with the cry, "Lord, I believe; help Thou mine unbelief." [See Mark 9:24.] You can never perish while you do this—never.[25]

Learn to trust in God. Learn to go to Him Who is mighty to save. He knows what you need before you ask Him; but He has made this your duty, and the duty of every one of us, to come to Him and ask Him in confidence for what we need. We must comply with the conditions laid down in his Word, namely, "ASK." Tell the dear Saviour just what you need. He that said, "Suffer little children to come unto Me, and forbid them not" [Luke 18:16], will not reject your prayer.[26] Prayer is the opening of the heart to God as to a friend. Not that it is necessary in order to make known to God what we are, but in order to enable us to receive Him. Prayer does not bring God down to us, but brings us up to Him.[27]

Repentance

The Bible does not teach that the sinner must repent before he can heed the invitation of Christ, "Come unto Me, all ye that labor and are heavy-laden, and I will give you rest." Matthew 11:28.[28] With the rich promises of the Bible before you, can you give place to doubt? Can you believe that when the poor sinner longs to return, longs to forsake his sins, the Lord sternly withholds him from coming to His feet in repentance? Away with such thoughts! Nothing can hurt your own soul more than to entertain such a conception of our Heavenly Father. He hates sin, but He loves the sinner, and He gave Himself in the person of Christ, that all who would might be saved and have eternal blessedness in the kingdom of Glory.[29]

Repentance as well as forgiveness is the gift of God through Christ. It is through the influence of the Holy Spirit that we are convinced of sin, and feel our need of pardon. None but the contrite are forgiven; but it is the grace of the Lord that makes the heart penitent. He is acquainted with all our weaknesses and infirmities, and He will help us. He will hear the prayer of faith; but the sincerity of prayer can be proved only by our efforts to bring ourselves into harmony with the great moral standard which will test every man's character. We need to open our hearts to the influence of the Spirit, and to experience its transforming power.[30]

Ask Him to give you repentance, to reveal Christ to you in His infinite love, in His perfect purity.... It is as we behold Him, as the light from our Saviour falls upon us, that we see the sinfulness of our

---

24–*Gospel Workers*, p. 261.
25–*The Desire of Ages*, p. 429.
26–*An Appeal to the Youth*, p. 55.
27–*Steps to Christ*, p. 93.

28–*Steps to Christ*, p. 26.
29–*Steps to Christ*, p. 54.
30–*The Review and Herald*, June 24, 1884.

own hearts.... When the light from Christ shines into our souls, we shall see how impure we are; we shall discern the selfishness of motive, the enmity against God, that has defiled every act of life. Then we shall know that our own righteousness is indeed as filthy rags, and that the blood of Christ alone can cleanse us from the defilement of sin, and renew our hearts in His Own likeness.[31] When men see their own nothingness, they are prepared to be clothed with the righteousness of Christ.[32] Beholding Christ means studying His life as given in His Word.... We are to fix our eyes upon Christ.... By beholding, we become changed—morally assimilated to the One who is perfect in character.[33]

A Firm Foundation

The hope of eternal life is not to be received upon slight grounds. It is a subject to be settled between God and your own soul—settled for eternity. A supposed hope, and nothing more, will prove your ruin. Since you are to stand or fall by the Word of God, it is to that Word you must look for testimony in your case. There you can see what is required of you to become a Christian.[34]

As with earnestness and assurance you come to God, tell Him all about your necessities. Claim His promises. He has given us the privilege of coming to Him, and we need have no fears of wearying Him. Do not doubt His Word of promise. Study the Word, and with your Bible in your hand say. "Here, Lord, I come to receive the gift Thou hast promised me." But you should be able to say, "I have done as Thou hast said." ... "And this is the promise that He hath promised us, even eternal life." [1 John 2:25.][35]

Give Yourself to Him

You have confessed your sins, and in heart put them away. You have resolved to give yourself to God. Now go to Him, and ask that He will wash away your sins and give you a new heart. Then believe that He does this because He has promised. This is the lesson which Jesus taught while He was on earth, that the gift which God promises us, we must believe we do receive, and it is ours.[36] Through faith each one should say, "The Lord my righteousness." When faith lays hold upon this gift, the praise of God will be upon our lips....[37] Let the language of each soul be, He is my Saviour, He died for me, and I hang my helpless soul upon Him. He is able to keep that which I have committed to His trust, against that day.[38] When we lay hold on the merit of Christ, and are able to say, "The Lord is my Saviour, my righteousness," then we are justified by faith, and have peace with God through our Lord Jesus Christ.[39]

31–*Steps to Christ*, pp. 28, 29.
32–*The Faith I Live By,* p. 111.
33–*Manuscript Releases*, vol. 12, p. 55.
34–*Testimonies for the Church*, vol. 1, pp. 163, 164.
35–*The Southern Watchman*, June 4, 1903.
36–*Steps to Christ*, p. 49.
37–*The Bible Echo*, April 1, 1893.
38–*The Signs of the Times*, September 15, 1887.
39–*The Signs of the Times*, November 10, 1890.

Written in Heaven

Christ came from the courts of glory to this sin-polluted world and humbled Himself to humanity. He identified Himself with our weaknesses and was tempted in all points like as we are. Christ perfected a righteous character here upon the earth, not on His own account, for His character was pure and spotless, but for fallen man. His character He offers to man if he will accept it. The sinner, through repentance of his sins, faith in Christ, and obedience to the perfect law of God, has the righteousness of Christ imputed to him; it becomes his righteousness, and his name is recorded in the Lamb's book of life. He becomes a child of God, a member of the royal family.[40]

---

[40]–*Testimonies for the Church*, vol. 3, pp. 371, 372.

Chapter 2

Rest in Christ

Resting in Joseph's Tomb

At last Jesus was at rest. The long day of shame and torture was ended. As the last rays of the setting sun ushered in the Sabbath, the Son of God lay in quietude in Joseph's tomb. His work completed, His hands folded in peace, He rested through the sacred hours of the Sabbath day.

The Passover was observed as it had been for centuries, while He to Whom it pointed had been slain by wicked hands, and lay in Joseph's tomb. On the Sabbath the courts of the Temple were filled with worshipers. The high priest from Golgotha was there, splendidly robed in his sacerdotal garments. White-turbaned priests, full of activity, performed their duties. But some present were not at rest as the blood of bulls and goats was offered for sin. They were not conscious that type had met Antitype, that an infinite sacrifice had been made for the sins of the world. They knew not that there was no further value in the performance of the ritual service. But never before had that service been witnessed with such conflicting feelings.[41]

Nicodemus, when he saw Jesus lifted up on the cross, remembered His words spoken by night in the Mount of Olives: "As Moses lifted up the serpent in the wilderness, even so must the Son of Man be lifted up: that whosoever believeth in Him should not perish, but have eternal life." John 3:14, 15. On that Sabbath, when Christ lay in the grave, Nicodemus had opportunity for reflection. A clearer light now illuminated his mind, and the words which Jesus had spoken to him were no longer mysterious. He felt that he had lost much by not connecting himself with the Saviour during His life. Now he recalled the events of Calvary. The prayer of Christ for His murderers and His answer to the petition of the dying thief spoke to the heart of the learned councilor. Again he looked upon the Saviour in His agony; again he heard that last cry, "It

---

41–*The Desire of Ages*, pp. 769, 770.

is finished" [John 19:30], spoken like the words of a conqueror. Again he beheld the reeling earth, the darkened heavens, the rent veil, the shivered rocks, and his faith was forever established. The very event that destroyed the hopes of the disciples convinced Joseph and Nicodemus of the divinity of Jesus. Their fears were overcome by the courage of a firm and unwavering faith.[42]

In the beginning the Father and the Son had rested upon the Sabbath after Their work of Creation. When "the heavens and the Earth were finished, and all the host of them" (Genesis 2:1), the Creator and all heavenly beings rejoiced in contemplation of the glorious scene. "The morning stars sang together, and all the sons of God shouted for joy." Job 38:7. Now Jesus rested from the work of redemption; and though there was grief among those who loved Him on Earth, yet there was joy in Heaven. Glorious to the eyes of heavenly beings was the promise of the future. A restored creation, a redeemed race, that having conquered sin could never fall,—this, the result to flow from Christ's completed work, God and angels saw. With this scene the day upon which Jesus rested is forever linked. For "His work is perfect;" and "whatsoever God doeth, it shall be forever." Deuteronomy 32:4; Ecclesiastes 3:14. When there shall be a "restitution of all things, which God hath spoken by the mouth of all His holy prophets since the world began" (Acts 3:21), the Creation Sabbath, the day on which Jesus lay at rest in Joseph's tomb, will still be a day of rest and rejoicing. Heaven and Earth will unite in praise, as "from one Sabbath to another" (Isaiah 66:23) the nations of the saved shall bow in joyful worship to God and the Lamb.[43]

While We Were Yet Sinners

"Herein is love, not that we loved God, but that He loved us, and sent His Son to be the propitiation for our sins" [1 John 4:10].... God permits His Son to be delivered up for our offenses. He Himself assumes toward the Sin-Bearer the character of a judge, divesting Himself of the endearing qualities of a father.

Herein His love commends itself in the most marvelous manner to the rebellious race. What a sight for angels to behold! What a hope for man, "that, while we were yet sinners, Christ died for us" [Romans 5:8]! The just suffered for the unjust; He bore our sins in His Own body on the tree. "He that spared not His Own Son, but delivered Him up for us all, how shall He not with Him also freely give us all things?" [Romans 8:32.][44]

He Is My Saviour

"The Word is nigh thee, even in thy mouth, and in thy heart: that is, the Word of faith, which we preach; That if thou shalt confess with thy mouth the Lord Jesus, and shalt believe in thine heart that God hath raised Him from the dead, thou shalt be saved. For with the heart man believeth unto righteousness; and with the mouth confession is made

---

42–*The Desire of Ages*, pp. 775, 776.
43–*The Desire of Ages*, p. 769.
44–*Testimonies to Ministers and Gospel Workers*, pp. 245, 246.

unto salvation."[45] The believing sinner is pronounced innocent, while the guilt is placed on Christ. The righteousness of Christ is placed on the debtor's account, and against his name on the balance sheet is written: Pardoned. Eternal Life.[46] God saves us under a law, that we must ask if we would receive, seek if we would find, and knock if we would have the door opened unto us.[47]

"This is the victory that overcometh the world, even our faith." [1 John 5:4.] Steadfast faith gives evidence that we are closely connected with the Saviour. Let us put away everything like fretfulness, and make melody in our hearts unto the Lord. Let us talk of His love, and sing of His grace and power. Faith will connect us with Him, and we shall be part of the Living Vine, and bear much fruit. We shall be patient and loving, and all the powers of our being will be devoted to God. Whatever gift you have, it is of God, and it should be given back to Him; but how many devote their God-given ability to the glorification of self! Christ wants us to come close to Himself, to accept the great sacrifice He has made for us. He is anxious to be our Helper, to bear our griefs and carry our sorrows. Will you let Him help you? Say to the world, "Jesus is my Saviour; He saves me today, making me His obedient child, and enabling me to keep all His commandments."[48] It is not enough to have a nominal faith. We must have faith that will appropriate the life-giving power to our souls. We suffer great loss because we do not exercise simple, living faith in Christ. We should be able to say, "He is my Saviour; He died for me; I look to Him as my complete Saviour and live."[49] If you can believe, all things are possible to him who believes.[50]

If you have this new birth you will delight yourself, not in the crooked ways of your own desires, but in the Lord. You will desire to be under His authority. You will strive constantly to reach a higher standard. Be not only Bible readers, but earnest Bible students, that you may know what God requires of you.[51]

"He that cometh unto Me, I will in no wise cast out" (John 6:37). If you have nothing else to plead before God but this one promise from your Lord and Saviour, you have the assurance that you will never, never be turned away. It may seem to you that you are hanging upon a single promise, but appropriate that one promise, and it will open to you the whole treasure house of the riches of the grace of Christ. Cling to that promise and you are safe. "Him that cometh unto Me I will in no wise cast out." Present this assurance to Jesus, and you are as safe as though inside the city of God.[52]

Changed Within

"Where sin abounded, grace did much more abound: That as sin hath reigned unto death, even so might grace reign through righteousness unto eternal life by Jesus Christ our Lord."[53] "For the

---

45–Romans 10:8–10.
46–*The Review and Herald*, August 24, 1897.
47–*Selected Messages*, book 1, p. 377.
48–*The Signs of the Times*, June 8, 1891.
49–*The Signs of the Times*, March 10, 1890.
50–Mark 9:23.
51–*Testimonies for the Church*, vol. 6, p. 161.
52–*Manuscript Releases*, vol. 10, p. 175.
53–Romans 5:20, 21.

love of Christ constraineth us."[54] "For it is God Which worketh in you both to will and to do of His good pleasure."[55]

Walk in the Spirit

Do not ... conclude that the upward path is the hard and the downward road is the easy way. All along the road that leads to death there are pains and penalties, there are sorrows and disappointments, there are warnings not to go on. God's love has made it hard for the heedless and headstrong to destroy themselves.... And all the way up the steep road leading to eternal life are wellsprings of joy to refresh the weary.[56]

"This I say then, Walk in the Spirit, and ye shall not fulfill the lust of the flesh. For the flesh lusteth against the Spirit, and the Spirit against the flesh: and these are contrary the one to the other: so that ye cannot do the things that ye would."[57] "If any man be in Christ, he is a new creature: old things are passed away; behold, all things are become new. And all things are of God...."[58] The plan of redemption contemplates our complete recovery from the power of Satan. Christ always separates the contrite soul from sin. He came to destroy the works of the Devil, and He has made provision that the Holy Spirit shall be imparted to every repentant soul, to keep him from sinning.[59]

In returning to God, the inclinations, the taste, the appetite, and the passions are brought into higher, holier channels. The bias to evil is overcome through man's determined effort, aided by the grace of Christ. The faculties that have been warped in a wrong direction are no longer misused, perverted, and misapplied. They are not wasted in selfish purposes, or fastened upon perishable things. The truth has been accepted, has convicted the soul, transformed the character, and there is a purification and elevation of all the powers of the being, and the God-given powers are no longer debased.[60] The experimental knowledge of God and of Christ transforms man into the image of God. It gives man the mastery of himself, bringing every impulse and passion of the lower nature under the control of the higher powers of the mind.[61]

No sooner did Zacchaeus yield to the influence of the Holy Spirit than he cast aside every practice contrary to integrity. No repentance is genuine that does not work reformation. The righteousness of Christ is not a cloak to cover unconfessed and unforsaken sin; it is a principle of life that transforms the character and controls the conduct. Holiness is wholeness for God; it is the entire surrender of heart and life to the indwelling of the principles of heaven.[62]

Enter His Rest

"Come unto Me, all ye that labor and are heavy-laden, and I will give you

---

54–2 Corinthians 5:14.
55–Philippians 2:13.
56–*Thoughts From the Mount of Blessing*, pp. 139, 140.
57–Galatians 5:16, 17.
58–2 Corinthians 5:17, 18.
59–*The Desire of Ages*, p. 311.

60–*The Review and Herald*, March 1, 1887.
61–*The Signs of the Times*, September 12, 1906.
62–*The Desire of Ages*, pp. 555, 556.

rest. Take My yoke upon you, and learn of Me; for I am meek and lowly in heart: and ye shall find rest unto your souls. For My yoke is easy, and My burden is light."[63] Those who have experience in wearing Christ's yoke of restraint and obedience know that it means to have rest and peace in Him.[64] The promise is, "Ye shall find rest unto your souls." There is rest, complete rest in abiding in Christ.[65] The Lord declares that when we diligently observe His Sabbath, it is a sign between Him and us, that we may know that He is the Lord that doth sanctify us. This knowledge is of more value to us than gold or silver or precious stones.[66]

"Fear thou not; for I am with thee: be not dismayed; for I am thy God: I will strengthen thee; yea, I will help thee; yea, I will uphold thee with the right hand of My righteousness." [Isaiah 41:10.] "Look unto Me, and be ye saved, all the ends of the Earth: for I am God, and there is none else." [Isaiah 45:22.] This is the message written in nature, which the Sabbath is appointed to keep in memory. When the Lord bade Israel hallow His Sabbaths, He said, "They shall be a sign between Me and you, that ye may know that I am Jehovah your God." [Ezekiel 20:20.][67]

"For we which have believed do enter into rest, as He said, As I have sworn in My wrath, if they shall enter into My rest: although the works were finished from the foundation of the world. For He spake in a certain place of the seventh day on this wise, And God did rest the seventh day from all His works. And in this place again, If they shall enter into My rest. Seeing therefore it remaineth that some must enter therein, and they to whom it was first preached entered not in because of unbelief: Again, He limiteth a certain day, saying in David, Today, after so long a time; as it is said, Today if ye will hear His voice, harden not your hearts. For if Jesus had given them rest, then would He not afterward have spoken of another day. There remaineth therefore a rest to the people of God. For he that is entered into His rest, he also hath ceased from his own works, as God did from His. Let us labor therefore to enter into that rest, lest any man fall after the same example of unbelief."[68] "Knowing that a man is not justified by the works of the law, but by the faith of Jesus Christ, even we have believed in Jesus Christ, that we might be justified by the faith of Christ, and not by the works of the law: for by the works of the law shall no flesh be justified."[69]

If you are willing to learn meekness and lowliness of heart in Christ's school, He will surely give you rest and peace. It is a terribly hard struggle to give up your own will and your own way. But this lesson learned, you will find rest and peace. Pride, selfishness, and ambition, must be overcome; your will must be swallowed up in the will of Christ. The whole life may become one constant love sacrifice, every action a manifestation, and every word an utterance of love. As the life of the vine circulates through stem and cluster, descends into the lower fibers, and reaches to the topmost leaf, so will the grace and love of Christ burn and abound in the

---

63–Matthew 11:28–30.
64–*Atlantic Union Gleaner*, September 9, 1903.
65–*That I May Know Him*, p. 45.
66–*General Conference Bulletin*, April 5, 1901.
67–*The Desire of Ages*, p. 282.

68–Hebrews 4:3–11.
69–Galatians 2:16.

soul, sending its virtues to every part of the being, and pervading every exercise of body and mind.

In being coworkers with Christ in the great work for which He gave His life, we shall find true rest. When we were sinners, He gave His life for us. He wants us to come to Him and learn of Him. Thus we are to find rest. He says He will give us rest. "Learn of Me; for I am meek and lowly in heart." [Matthew 11:29.] In doing this you will find in your own experience the rest that Christ gives, the rest that comes from wearing His yoke and lifting His burdens.

A form of godliness without the power is a weariness and burden; but when the whole heart is enlisted in the service of Christ, there is rest to the soul; for God causeth such to triumph daily over the powers of darkness. God helps him who commits his soul unto the Lord as unto a faithful Creator.[70]

---

[70]–*Sons and Daughters of God*, p. 76.

Chapter 3

Devotion

Breathing

Prayer is the breath of the soul. It is the secret of spiritual power. No other means of grace can be substituted, and the health of the soul be preserved.[71] Religion must begin with emptying and purifying the heart, and must be nurtured by daily prayer. [72] Daily prayer is as essential to growth in grace, and even to spiritual life itself, as is temporal food to physical well-being. [73] Let not your daily labor keep you from this duty. Take time to pray. And as you pray, believe that God hears you, have faith mixed with your prayers. Let faith take hold of the blessing, and it is yours.[74] Morning and evening your earnest prayers should ascend to God for His blessing and guidance. True prayer takes hold upon Omnipotence and gives us the victory.

Upon his knees the Christian obtains strength to resist temptation.[75]

As a man [Christ] supplicated the throne of God, until His humanity was charged with a heavenly current that connected humanity with divinity.[76] In a world of sin Jesus endured struggles and torture of soul. In communion with God He could unburden the sorrows that were crushing Him. Here He found comfort and joy.[77] It was in hours of solitary prayer that Jesus in His Earth life received wisdom and power. Let the youth follow His example in finding at dawn and twilight a quiet season for communion with their Father in Heaven. And throughout the day let them lift up their hearts to God.[78]

The Reading of the Word

The reading of the Word of God prepares the mind for prayer. One of the

---

71–*Gospel Workers*, pp. 254, 255.
72–*Testimonies for the Church*, vol. 4, p. 535.
73–*The Review and Herald*, May 3, 1881.
74–*The Signs of the Times*, November 18, 1886.

75–*Testimonies for the Church*, vol. 4, pp. 615, 616.
76–*The Signs of the Times*, June 7, 1905.
77–*The Desire of Ages*, p. 362.
78–*Education*, p. 259.

greatest reasons why many have so little disposition to draw near to God by prayer is, that they have unfitted themselves for this sacred work by reading fascinating stories, which have excited the imagination and aroused unholy passions. The Word of God becomes distasteful; the hour of prayer is not thought of.[79]

Communion With God

In order to commune with God, we must have something to say to Him concerning our actual life.[80] Jesus taught His disciples that only that prayer which arises from unfeigned lips, prompted by the actual wants of the soul, is genuine, and will bring Heaven's blessing to the petitioner.[81] It is our privilege to open our hearts, and let the sunshine of Christ's presence in.[82] Daily prayer is as essential to growth in grace, and even to spiritual life itself, as is temporal food to physical well-being.[83] Communion with God is highly essential for spiritual health, and here only may be obtained that wisdom and correct judgment so necessary in the performance of every duty.[84] Day by day, morning and evening, the humble heart needs to offer up prayers to which will be returned answers of grace and peace and joy.[85]

Our Saviour identified Himself with our needs and weakness, in that He became a suppliant, a petitioner, seeking from His Father fresh supplies of strength, that He might come forth braced for duty and trial.[86] The early morning often found Him in some secluded place, meditating, searching the Scriptures, or in prayer. From these quiet hours He would return to His home to take up His duties again, and to give an example of patient toil.[87]

All who are under the training of God need the quiet hour for communion with their own hearts, with nature, and with God. In them is to be revealed a life that is not in harmony with the world, its customs, or its practices; and they need to have a personal experience in obtaining a knowledge of the will of God. We must individually hear Him speaking to the heart. When every other voice is hushed, and in quietness we wait before Him, the silence of the soul makes more distinct the voice of God. He bids us, "Be still, and know that I am God." Psalm 46:10. This is the effectual preparation for all labor for God. Amidst the hurrying throng, and the strain of life's intense activities, he who is thus refreshed will be surrounded with an atmosphere of light and peace. He will receive a new endowment of both physical and mental strength. His life will breathe out a fragrance, and will reveal a divine power that will reach men's hearts.[88]

The First Work

In order to attain to this high calling of God in Christ Jesus, you must begin

---

79–*The Review and Herald*, March 11, 1880.
80–*The Signs of the Times*, August 14, 1884.
81–*The Signs of the Times*, December 3, 1896.
82–*Sons and Daughters of God*, p. 199.
83–*The Review and Herald*, May 3, 1881.
84–*Testimonies for the Church*, vol. 4, p. 459.
85–*Our High Calling*, p. 50.

86–*Steps to Christ*, p. 93.
87–*The Desire of Ages*, p. 89.
88–*The Ministry of Healing*, p. 58.

the day with your Saviour. The very first out-breathing of the soul in the morning should be for the presence of Jesus. "Without Me," He says, "ye can do nothing." [John 15:5.] It is Jesus that we need; His light, His life, His Spirit, must be ours continually. We need Him every hour. And we should pray in the morning that as the sun illuminates the landscape, and fills the world with light, so the Sun of Righteousness may shine into the chambers of mind and heart, and make us all light in the Lord. We cannot do without His presence one moment.[89]

Consecrate yourself to God in the morning; make this your very first work. Let your prayer be, "Take me, O Lord, as wholly Thine. I lay all my plans at Thy feet. Use me today in Thy service. Abide with me, and let all my work be wrought in Thee." This is a daily matter. Each morning consecrate yourself to God for that day. Surrender all your plans to Him, to be carried out or given up as His providence shall indicate. Thus day by day you may be giving your life into the hands of God, and thus your life will be molded more and more after the life of Christ.[90] When you rise in the morning, kneel at your bedside, and ask God to give you strength to fulfill the duties of the day, and to meet its temptations. Ask Him to help you to bring into your work Christ's sweetness of character. Ask Him to help you to speak words that will inspire those around you with hope and courage, and draw you nearer to the Saviour.[91]

The trials and privations of which so many youth complain, Christ endured without murmuring. And this discipline is the very experience the youth need, which will give firmness to their character, and make them like Christ, strong in spirit to resist temptation. They will not, if they separate from the influence of those who would lead them astray and corrupt their morals, be overcome by the devices of Satan. Through daily prayer to God, they will have wisdom and grace from Him to bear the conflicts and stern realities of life, and come off victorious. Fidelity, and serenity of mind, can only be retained by watchfulness and prayer.[92]

Life of the Soul

Secret prayer ... is the life of the soul. It is impossible for the soul to flourish while prayer is neglected. Family or public prayer alone is not sufficient. In solitude let the soul be laid open to the inspecting eye of God.... In secret prayer the soul is free from surrounding influences, free from excitement. Calmly, yet fervently, will it reach out after God. Sweet and abiding will be the influence emanating from Him Who seeth in secret, Whose ear is open to hear the prayer arising from the heart. By calm, simple faith the soul holds communion with God and gathers to itself rays of divine light to strengthen and sustain it in the conflict with Satan.[93]

Prepared for the Day

Those who will put on the whole armor of God and devote some time every day to meditation and prayer and

---

89–*The Bible Echo*, January 15, 1892.
90–*Steps to Christ*, p. 70.
91–*The Review and Herald*, May 5, 1910.

92–*The Youth's Instructor*, March 1, 1872.
93–*Steps to Christ*, p. 98.

to the study of the Scriptures will be connected with Heaven and will have a saving, transforming influence upon those around them. Great thoughts, noble aspirations, clear perceptions of truth and duty to God, will be theirs. They will be yearning for purity, for light, for love, for all the graces of heavenly birth. Their earnest prayers will enter into that within the veil. This class will have a sanctified boldness to come into the presence of the Infinite One. They will feel that Heaven's light and glories are for them, and they will become refined, elevated, ennobled by this intimate acquaintance with God.[94]

The strength acquired in prayer to God, united with individual effort in training the mind to thoughtfulness and care-taking, prepares the person for daily duties and keeps the spirit in peace under all circumstances, however trying.

The temptations to which we are daily exposed make prayer a necessity.[95] Every worker who follows the example of Christ will be prepared to receive and use the power that God has promised to His church for the ripening of Earth's harvest. Morning by morning, as the heralds of the Gospel kneel before the Lord and renew their vows of consecration to Him, He will grant them the presence of His Spirit, with Its reviving, sanctifying power. As they go forth to the day's duties, they have the assurance that the unseen agency of the Holy Spirit enables them to be "laborers together with God."[96]

94–*Testimonies for the Church*, vol. 5, pp. 112, 113.

95–*Testimonies for the Church*, vol. 4, p. 459.
96–*The Acts of the Apostles*, p. 56.

Chapter 4

The Word

Habits of Devotion

Every morning dedicate yourself, soul, body, and spirit, to God. Establish habits of devotion and trust more and more in your Saviour. You may believe with all confidence that the Lord Jesus loves you and wishes you to grow up to His stature of character. He wishes you to grow in His love, to increase and strengthen in all the fullness of divine love.[97] Go daily to the Lord for instruction and guidance; depend upon God for light and knowledge. Pray for this instruction and this light until you get it.[98] Let much time be spent in prayer and close searching of the Word.[99]

The reading of the Word of God prepares the mind for prayer. One of the greatest reasons why many have so little disposition to draw near to God by prayer is, that they have unfitted themselves for this sacred work by reading fascinating stories, which have excited the imagination and aroused unholy passions. The Word of God becomes distasteful; the hour of prayer is not thought of. Prayer is the strength of the Christian. When alone, he is not alone; he feels the presence of One Who has said, "Lo, I am with you alway." [Matthew 28:20.][100]

Let us turn aside from the dusty, heated thoroughfares of life to rest in the shadow of Christ's love, and learn from Him the lesson of quiet trust. Not a pause for a moment in His presence, but personal contact with Christ, to sit down in companionship with Him,—this is our need. Many, even in their seasons of devotion, fail of receiving the blessing of real communion with God. They are in too great haste. With hurried steps they press through the circle of Christ's loving presence, pausing perhaps a moment within the sacred precincts, but not waiting for counsel. They have no time to remain with the divine Teacher. With their burdens they return to their

---

97–*Mind, Character, and Personality*, vol. 1, p. 15.
98–*The Review and Herald*, July 1, 1909.
99–*Testimonies for the Church*, vol. 6, p. 65.

100–*The Review and Herald*, March 11, 1880.

work.[101] Christians must ... take time for contemplation, for prayer, and the study of the Word of God. It will not do to be always under the strain of the work and excitement, for in this way personal piety is neglected, and the powers of mind and body are injured.[102]

The Word of the Living God

It is one thing to treat the Bible as a book of good moral instruction, to be heeded so far as is consistent with the spirit of the times and our position in the world; it is another thing to regard it as it really is—the Word of the living God, the Word that is our life, the Word that is to mold our actions, our words, and our thoughts. To hold God's Word as anything less than this is to reject it.[103]

Never should the Bible be studied without prayer. Before opening its pages we should ask for the enlightenment of the Holy Spirit, and it will be given. When Nathanael came to Jesus, the Saviour exclaimed, "Behold an Israelite indeed, in whom is no guile!" Nathanael said, "Whence knowest Thou me?" Jesus answered, "Before that Philip called thee, when thou wast under the fig tree, I saw thee." John 1:47, 48. And Jesus will see us also in the secret places of prayer if we will seek Him for light that we may know what is truth. Angels from the world of light will be with those who in humility of heart seek for divine guidance.[104]

There is nothing more calculated to strengthen the intellect than the study of the Scriptures. No other book is so potent to elevate the thoughts, to give vigor to the faculties, as the broad, ennobling truths of the Bible. If God's Word were studied as it should be, men would have a breadth of mind, a nobility of character, and a stability of purpose rarely seen in these times.[105]

Our Daily Bread

Jesus declares, "Except ye eat the flesh of the Son of Man, and drink His blood, ye have no life in you." And He explains Himself by saying, "The words that I speak unto you, they are Spirit, and they are life." John 6:53, 63. Our bodies are built up from what we eat and drink; and as in the natural economy, so in the spiritual economy: it is what we meditate upon that will give tone and strength to our spiritual nature.[106] The prayer for daily bread includes not only food to sustain the body, but that spiritual bread which will nourish the soul unto life everlasting. Jesus ... says, "I am the living Bread which came down from Heaven: if any man eat of this bread, he shall live forever." [John 6:51.] Our Saviour is the Bread of life, and it is by beholding His love, by receiving it into the soul, that we feed upon the Bread Which came down from Heaven.

We receive Christ through His Word, and the Holy Spirit is given to open the Word of God to our understanding, and bring home its truths to our hearts. We are to pray day by day that as we read

---

101–*The Signs of the Times*, July 6, 1904.
102–*The Review and Herald*, November 7, 1893.
103–*Education*, p. 260.
104–*Steps to Christ*, p. 91.

105–*Steps to Christ*, p. 90.
106–*Steps to Christ*, p. 88.

His Word, God will send His Spirit to reveal to us the truth that will strengthen our souls for the day's need.... In this communion with Christ, through prayer and the study of the great and precious truths of His Word, we shall as hungry souls be fed; as those that thirst, we shall be refreshed at the Fountain of life.[107]

Daily pray for the light of the Holy Spirit to shine upon the pages of the Sacred Book, [to] be enabled to comprehend the things of the Spirit of God. We must have implicit trust in God's Word, or we are lost.... "God hath from the beginning chosen you to salvation through sanctification of the Spirit and belief of the truth." [2 Thessalonians 2:13.] In this text the two agencies in the salvation of man are revealed,—the divine influence, the strong, living faith of those who follow Christ. It is through the sanctification of the Spirit and the belief of the truth that we become laborers together with God.[108] It would be well for us to spend a thoughtful hour each day in contemplation of the life of Christ. We should take it point by point, and let the imagination grasp each scene, especially the closing ones. As we thus dwell upon His great sacrifice for us, our confidence in Him will be more constant, our love will be quickened, and we shall be more deeply imbued with His Spirit. If we would be saved at last, we must learn the lesson of penitence and humiliation at the foot of the cross.[109]

Appreciate His Character

The Gospel is the power of God and the wisdom of God. The character of Christ on Earth revealed divinity, and the Gospel which He has given is to be the study of His human heritage.... The Word is to be respected and obeyed. That Book which contains the record of Christ's life, His work, His doctrines, His sufferings, and final triumphs, is to be the source of our strength.[110] Through the sanctification of the truth man becomes a partaker of the divine nature, having escaped the corruption that is in the world through lust.[111] The law of love being the foundation of the government of God, the happiness of all intelligent beings depends upon their perfect accord with its great principles of righteousness. God desires from all His creatures the service of love—service that springs from an appreciation of His character. He takes no pleasure in a forced obedience; and to all He grants freedom of will, that they may render Him voluntary service.[112]

God speaks to us in His Word. Here we have in clearer lines the revelation of His character, of His dealings with men, and the great work of redemption. Here is open before us the history of patriarchs and prophets and other holy men of old. They were men "subject to like passions as we are." James 5:17. We see how they struggled through discouragements like our own, how they fell under temptation as we have done, and yet took heart again and conquered through the grace of God; and, beholding, we are encouraged in

---

107–*Thoughts From the Mount of Blessing*, pp. 112, 113.
108–*The Review and Herald*, December 1, 1891.
109–*The Desire of Ages*, p. 83.
110–*Selected Messages*, book 1, p. 245.
111–*The Review and Herald*, March 1, 1887.
112–*Patriarchs and Prophets*, p. 34.

our striving after righteousness. As we read of the precious experiences granted them, of the light and love and blessing it was theirs to enjoy, and of the work they wrought through the grace given them, the Spirit that inspired them kindles a flame of holy emulation in our hearts and a desire to be like them in character— like them to walk with God.[113]

Written on the Heart

The "new covenant" was established upon "better promises,"—the promise of forgiveness of sins, and of the grace of God to renew the heart, and bring it into harmony with the principles of God's law. "This shall be the covenant that I will make with the house of Israel: After those days, saith the Lord, I will put My law in their inward parts, and write it in their hearts." [Jeremiah 31:33.][114] He has given us His Word to point out the way of life, and He has not left us simply to carry that Word, but has also promised to give it efficiency by the power of the Holy Spirit. Is there need, then, that any should walk in uncertainty, grieving that they do not know and experience the movings of the Holy Spirit upon their hearts? Are you hungering and thirsting for instruction in righteousness? Then you have the sure promise that you shall be filled.[115]

Behold the Lamb

All those who look to Him with undivided hearts, He will greatly bless. Those who have thus looked to Him have caught more distinct views of Jesus as their Sin-Bearer, their all-sufficient Sacrifice, and have been hid in the cleft of the rock, to behold the Lamb of God Who taketh away the sins of the world. When we have a sense of His all-sufficient sacrifice, our lips are tuned to the highest, loftiest themes of praise.[116] The brazen serpent, lifted upon a pole, illustrates the Son of God, Who was to die upon the cross. The people who are suffering from the effects of sin can find hope and salvation alone in the provision God has made. As the Israelites saved their lives by looking upon the brazen serpent, so sinners can look to Christ and live.[117] Beholding Christ means studying His life as given in His Word…. We are to fix our eyes upon Christ…. By beholding, we become changed—morally assimilated to the One who is perfect in character.[118]

We should meditate upon the Scriptures, thinking soberly and candidly upon the things that pertain to our eternal salvation. The infinite mercy and love of Jesus, the sacrifice made in our behalf, call for most serious and solemn reflection. We should dwell upon the character of our dear Redeemer and Intercessor. We should seek to comprehend the meaning of the plan of salvation. We should meditate upon the mission of Him Who came to save His people from their sins. By constantly contemplating heavenly themes,

---

113–*Steps to Christ*, pp. 87, 88.
114–*The Review and Herald*, October 17, 1907.
115–*Testimonies to Ministers and Gospel Workers*, p. 199.

116–*Special Testimonies on Education*, p. 78.
117–*The Spirit of Prophecy*, vol. 1, p. 318.
118–*Manuscript Releases*, vol. 12, p. 55.

our faith and love will grow stronger. Our prayers will be more and more acceptable to God, because they will be more and more mixed with faith and love. They will be more intelligent and fervent. There will be more constant confidence in Jesus, and you will have a daily, living experience in the willingness and power of Christ to save unto the uttermost all that come unto God by Him.[119]

As we meditate upon the perfections of our divine Model, we shall desire to become wholly transformed and renewed in the image of His purity. There will be a hungering and thirsting of soul to be made like Him Whom we adore. The more our thoughts are upon Christ, the more we shall speak of Him to others, and represent Him to the world.[120] When a man turns away from human imperfections, and beholds Jesus, a divine transformation takes place in his character. He fixes his eye upon Christ as on a mirror which reflects the glory of God, and by beholding, he becomes "changed into the same image." [2 Corinthians 3:18.][121] The wisdom of God enlightens his mind, and he beholds wondrous things out of His law. As a man is converted by the truth, the work of transformation of character goes on. He has an increased measure of understanding. In becoming a man of obedience to God, he has the mind of Christ, and the will of God becomes his will.[122]

When we study the divine character in the light of the cross we see mercy, tenderness, and forgiveness blended with equity and justice. We see in the midst of the throne One bearing in hands and feet and side the marks of the suffering endured to reconcile man to God. We see a Father, infinite, dwelling in light unapproachable, yet receiving us to Himself through the merits of His Son. The cloud of vengeance that threatened only misery and despair, in the light reflected from the cross reveals the writing of God: Live, sinner, live! ye penitent, believing souls, live! I have paid a ransom.[123]

119–*The Review and Herald*, June 12, 1888.
120–*The Review and Herald*, June 12, 1888.
121–*This Day With God*, p. 46
122–*The Signs of the Times*, January 2, 1907.
123–*The Acts of the Apostles*, p. 333.

Chapter 5

Prayer Life

Spiritual Life

In order to have spiritual life and energy, we must have actual intercourse with our Heavenly Father. Our minds may be drawn out toward Him; we may meditate upon His works, His mercies, His blessings; but this is not, in the fullest sense, communing with Him.[124] What we need is a deep, individual heart and soul experience.[125] Daily prayer is as essential to growth in grace, and even to spiritual life itself, as is temporal food to physical well-being. We should accustom ourselves to often lift the thoughts to God in prayer. If the mind wanders, we must bring it back; by persevering effort, habit will finally make it easy.[126] Prayer is a necessity; for it is the life of the soul.[127] Prayer is the strength of the Christian. When alone, he is not alone; he feels the presence of One Who has said, "Lo, I am with you always." [Matthew 28:20.][128]

We should go to Jesus and tell Him all our needs. We may bring Him our little cares and perplexities as well as our greater troubles. Whatever arises to disturb or distress us, we should take it to the Lord in prayer. When we feel that we need the presence of Christ at every step, Satan will have little opportunity to intrude his temptations.... We should make no one our confidant but Jesus. We can safely commune with Him of all that is in our hearts.[129]

We should now acquaint ourselves with God by proving His promises. Angels record every prayer that is earnest and sincere. We should rather dispense with selfish gratifications than neglect communion with God. The deepest poverty, the greatest self-denial, with His approval, is better than riches, honors, ease, and friendship without it. We must

---

124–*Steps to Christ*, p. 93.
125–*The Review and Herald*, July 1, 1909.
126–*Messages to Young People*, p. 115.
127–*Education*, p. 258.

128–*The Review and Herald*, March 11, 1880.
129–*Testimonies for the Church*, vol. 5, pp. 200, 201.

take time to pray.[130] Look unto Jesus in simplicity and faith. Gaze upon Jesus until the spirit faints under the excess of light. We do not half pray. We do not half believe. "Ask, and it shall be given you." Luke 11:9. Pray, believe, strengthen one another. Pray as you never before prayed that the Lord will lay His hand upon you, that you may be able to comprehend the length and breadth and depth and height, and to know the love of Christ, which passeth knowledge, that you may be filled with all the fullness of God.[131]

Our prayers should be full of tenderness and love. When we yearn for a deeper, broader realization of the Saviour's love, we shall cry to God for more wisdom.... O that we could see as we should the necessity of seeking the Lord with all the heart! Then we should find Him. May God teach His people how to pray.... Then they will pray with earnestness, and their requests will be heard and answered.[132]

There is now need of much prayer. Christ commands, "Pray without ceasing" [1 Thessalonians 5:17]; that is, keep the mind uplifted to God, the Source of all power and efficiency.[133] Let the soul be drawn out and upward, that God may grant us a breath of the heavenly atmosphere.[134] Let much time be spent in prayer and close searching of the word.[135] Those whose hearts are open to receive the support and blessing of God will walk in a holier atmosphere than that of earth and will have constant communion with heaven.[136]

Several Times a Day

In order to attain to this high calling of God in Christ Jesus, you must begin the day with your Saviour. The very first out-breathing of the soul in the morning should be for the presence of Jesus. "Without me," He says, "ye can do nothing." [John 15:5.] It is Jesus that we need; His light, His life, His Spirit, must be ours continually. We need Him every hour. And we should pray in the morning that as the sun illuminates the landscape, and fills the world with light, so the Sun of Righteousness may shine into the chambers of mind and heart, and make us all light in the Lord. We cannot do without His presence one moment.[137]

While God condemns a mere round of ceremonies, without the spirit of worship, He looks with great pleasure upon those who love Him, bowing morning and evening to seek pardon for sins committed and to present their requests for needed blessings.[138] Morning and evening your earnest prayers should ascend to God for His blessing and guidance. True prayer takes hold upon Omnipotence and gives us the victory. Upon his knees the Christian obtains strength to resist temptation.[139] Several times each day precious, golden moments should be consecrated to prayer and the study of the Scriptures,

---

130–*The Great Controversy*, p. 622.
131–*Testimonies for the Church*, vol. 7, p. 214.
132–*Gospel Workers*, p. 178.
133–*The Review and Herald*, March 2, 1897.
134–*Steps to Christ*, p. 99.
135–*General Conference Daily Bulletin*, March 2, 1899.
136–*Steps to Christ*, p. 99.
137–*The Bible Echo*, January 15, 1892.
138–*Patriarchs and Prophets*, p. 354.
139–*Testimonies for the Church*, vol. 4, pp. 615, 616.

if it is only to commit a text to memory, that spiritual life may exist in the soul. The varied interests of the cause furnish us with food for reflection and inspiration for our prayers. Communion with God is highly essential for spiritual health, and here only may be obtained that wisdom and correct judgment so necessary in the performance of every duty.[140]

Our need of Christ's intercession is constant. Day by day, morning and evening, the humble heart needs to offer up prayers to which will be returned answers of grace and peace and joy.[141] It is just as convenient, just as essential, for us to pray three times a day as it was for Daniel. Prayer is the life of the soul, the foundation of spiritual growth. In your home, before your family, and before your workmen, you should testify to this truth. And when you are privileged to meet with your brethren in the church, tell them of the necessity of keeping open the channel of communication between God and the soul. Tell them that if they will find heart and voice to pray, God will find answers to their prayers. Tell them not to neglect their religious duties. Exhort the brethren to pray. We must seek if we would find, we must ask if we would receive, we must knock if we would have the door opened unto us.[142]

Deliver Us From Evil

As activity increases and men become successful in doing any work for God, there is danger of trusting to human plans and methods. There is a tendency to pray less, and to have less faith. Like the disciples, we are in danger of losing sight of our dependence on God, and seeking to make a savior of our activity. We need to look constantly to Jesus, realizing that it is His power which does the work. While we are to labor earnestly for the salvation of the lost, we must also take time for meditation, for prayer, and for the study of the Word of God. Only the work accomplished with much prayer, and sanctified by the merit of Christ, will in the end prove to have been efficient for good.[143] You need to watch, lest the busy activities of life lead you to neglect prayer when you most need the strength prayer would give.[144] Neglect the exercise of prayer, or engage in prayer spasmodically, now and then, as it is deemed convenient, and you lose your connection with God. The Christian life becomes dry, and the spiritual faculties have no vitality. The religious experience lacks health and vigor.[145]

The only reason for our lack of power with God is to be found in ourselves. If the inner life of many who profess the truth were presented before them, they would not claim to be Christians. They are not growing in grace. A hurried prayer is offered now and then, but there is no real communion with God. We must be much in prayer if we would make progress in the divine life.[146]

All who do not earnestly search the Scriptures and submit every desire and purpose of life to that unerring test, all who do not seek God in prayer for a

---

140–*Testimonies for the Church*, vol. 4, p. 459.
141–*Our High Calling,* p. 50.
142–*The Signs of the Times*, February 10, 1890.
143–*The Desire of Ages*, p. 362.
144–*Testimonies for the Church*, vol. 5, p. 560.
145–*The Signs of the Times*, July 31, 1893.
146–*Testimonies for the Church*, vol. 5, p. 161.

knowledge of His will, will surely wander from the right path and fall under the deception of Satan.[147] The darkness of the evil one encloses those who neglect to pray. The whispered temptations of the enemy entice them to sin; and it is all because they do not make use of the privileges that God has given them in the divine appointment of prayer.... Without unceasing prayer and diligent watching we are in danger of growing careless and of deviating from the right path. The adversary seeks continually to obstruct the way to the mercy seat, that we may not by earnest supplication and faith obtain grace and power to resist temptation.[148]

The temptations to which we are daily exposed make prayer a necessity. In order that we may be kept by the power of God through faith, the desires of the mind should be continually ascending in silent prayer. When we are surrounded by influences calculated to lead us away from God, our petitions for help and strength must be unwearied. Unless, this is so, we shall never be successful in breaking down pride and overcoming the power of temptation to sinful indulgences which keep us from the Saviour.[149] The enemy knows when we undertake to do without our Lord, and he is there, ready to fill our minds with his evil suggestions that we may fall from our steadfastness.[150]

The experience of the disciples in the Garden of Gethsemane contains a lesson for the Lord's people today.... They had not heeded the repeated warning, "Watch and pray." [Matthew 26:41.] At first they had been much troubled to see their Master, usually so calm and dignified, wrestling with a sorrow that was beyond comprehension. They had prayed as they heard the strong cries of the divine-human Sufferer. They did not intend to forsake their Lord, but they seemed paralyzed by a stupor which they might have shaken off if they had continued pleading with God. They did not realize the necessity of watchfulness and earnest prayer in order to withstand temptation.[151]

Without unceasing prayer and diligent watching, we are in danger of growing careless, and of deviating from the right path.[152] Spiritual vigilance on our part individually is the price of safety.[153] What a wonder it is that we pray so little! God is ready and willing to hear the sincere prayer of the humblest of His children, and yet there is much manifest reluctance on our part to make known our wants to God. What can the angels of Heaven think of poor helpless human beings, who are subject to temptation, when God's heart of infinite love yearns toward them, ready to give them more than they can ask or think, and yet they pray so little and have so little faith?[154] The victory is not won without much earnest prayer, without the humbling of self at every step.[155]

Pray, yes, pray as you have never prayed before, that you may not be deluded by Satan's devices, that you may not be given up to a heedless, careless, vain spirit, and attend to religious duties

---

147–*Testimonies for the Church*, vol. 5, p. 192.
148–*Steps to Christ*, pp. 94, 95.
149–*The Youth's Instructor*, August 18, 1898.
150–*The Bible Echo*, January 15, 1892.
151–*The Review and Herald*, July 7, 1910.
152–*The Review and Herald*, December 8, 1904.
153–Letter 47, 1893.
154–*Steps to Christ*, p. 94.
155–*Thoughts From the Mount of Blessing*, p. 142.

to quiet your own conscience.[156] When we feel the least inclined to commune with Jesus, let us pray the most. By so doing we shall break Satan's snare, the clouds of darkness will disappear, and we shall realize the sweet presence of Jesus. Let us here resolve that we will not sin against God with our lips, that we will never speak in a light and trifling manner, that we will never murmur or complain at the providence of God, and that we will not become accusers of our brethren.... If all would labor to repress sinful thoughts and feelings, giving them no expression in words or acts, Satan would be defeated; for he would not know how to prepare his specious temptations to meet their case[157]

God designs that every one of us shall be perfect in Him, so that we may represent to the world the perfection of His character. He wants us to be set free from sin, that we may not disappoint Heaven, that we may not grieve our divine Redeemer. He does not desire us to profess Christianity, and yet not avail ourselves of that grace which is able to make us perfect, that we may be found wanting in nothing, but unblamable before Him in love and holiness.[158]

Answered Prayer

There are certain conditions upon which we may expect that God will hear and answer our prayers. One of the first of these is that we feel our need of help from Him. He has promised, "I will pour water upon him that is thirsty, and floods upon the dry ground." Isaiah 44:3. Those who hunger and thirst after righteousness, who long after God, may be sure that they will be filled. The heart must be open to the Spirit's influence, or God's blessing cannot be received.

Our great need is itself an argument and pleads most eloquently in our behalf. But the Lord is to be sought unto to do these things for us. He says, "Ask, and it shall be given you." And "He that spared not His Own Son, but delivered Him up for us all, how shall He not with Him also freely give us all things?" Matthew 7:7; Romans 8:32.

If we regard iniquity in our hearts, if we cling to any known sin, the Lord will not hear us; but the prayer of the penitent, contrite soul is always accepted. When all known wrongs are righted, we may believe that God will answer our petitions. Our own merit will never commend us to the favor of God; it is the worthiness of Jesus that will save us, His blood that will cleanse us; yet we have a work to do in complying with the conditions of acceptance.

Another element of prevailing prayer is faith. "He that cometh to God must believe that He is, and that He is a rewarder of them that diligently seek Him." Hebrews 11:6. Jesus said to His disciples, "What things soever ye desire, when ye pray, believe that ye receive them, and ye shall have them." Mark 11:24. Do we take Him at His word?

The assurance is broad and unlimited, and He is faithful Who has promised. When we do not receive the very things we asked for, at the time we ask, we are still to believe that the Lord hears and

---

156–*Testimonies for the Church*, vol. 2, p. 144.
157–*Historical Sketches of the Foreign Missions of the Seventh-day Adventists*, p. 146.
158–*The Bible Echo*, January 15, 1892.

that He will answer our prayers. We are so erring and short-sighted that we sometimes ask for things that would not be a blessing to us, and our Heavenly Father in love answers our prayers by giving us that which will be for our highest good—that which we ourselves would desire if with vision divinely enlightened we could see all things as they really are. When our prayers seem not to be answered, we are to cling to the promise; for the time of answering will surely come, and we shall receive the blessing we need most. But to claim that prayer will always be answered in the very way and for the particular thing that we desire, is presumption. God is too wise to err, and too good to withhold any good thing from them that walk uprightly. Then do not fear to trust Him, even though you do not see the immediate answer to your prayers. Rely upon His sure promise, "Ask, and it shall be given you."

If we take counsel with our doubts and fears, or try to solve everything that we cannot see clearly, before we have faith, perplexities will only increase and deepen. But if we come to God, feeling helpless and dependent, as we really are, and in humble, trusting faith make known our wants to Him Whose knowledge is infinite, Who sees everything in creation, and who governs everything by His will and word, He can and will attend to our cry, and will let light shine into our hearts. Through sincere prayer we are brought into connection with the mind of the Infinite. We may have no remarkable evidence at the time that the face of our Redeemer is bending over us in compassion and love, but this is even so. We may not feel His visible touch, but His hand is upon us in love and pitying tenderness.[159]

---

[159]–*Steps to Christ*, pp. 95, 96.

Chapter 6

Faith, Prayer, and the Power of the Word

The Gift of Faith

Faith is trusting in God,—believing that He loves us, and knows what is for our best good. Thus, instead of our own way, it leads us to choose His way. In place of our ignorance, it accepts His wisdom; in place of our weakness, His strength; in place of our sinfulness, His righteousness. Our lives, ourselves, are already His; faith acknowledges His ownership, and accepts its blessings. Truth, uprightness, purity, are pointed out as secrets of life's success. It is faith that puts us in possession of these. Every good impulse or aspiration is the gift of God; faith receives from God the life that alone can produce true growth and efficiency.[160] Faith that enables us to receive God's gifts is itself a gift, of which some measure is imparted to every human being.

It grows as exercised in appropriating the Word of God. In order to strengthen faith, we must often bring it in contact with the Word.[161]

If we take counsel with our doubts and fears, or try to solve everything that we cannot see clearly, before we have faith, perplexities will only increase and deepen. But if we come to God, feeling helpless and dependent, as we really are, and in humble, trusting faith make known our wants to Him Whose knowledge is infinite, Who sees everything in creation, and Who governs everything by His will and word, He can and will attend to our cry, and will let light shine into our hearts. Through sincere prayer we are brought into connection with the mind of the Infinite. We may have no remarkable evidence at the time that the face of our Redeemer is bending over us in compassion and love, but this is even so. We may

---

160–*Gospel Workers*, p. 259.

161–*Education*, pp. 253, 254.

not feel His visible touch, but His hand is upon us in love and pitying tenderness.[162]

Ask

When Jesus was upon the Earth, He taught His disciples how to pray. He directed them to present their daily needs before God, and to cast all their care upon Him. And the assurance He gave them that their petitions should be heard, is assurance also to us.[163] Jesus healed the people of their diseases when they had faith in His power; He helped them in the things which they could see, thus inspiring them with confidence in Him concerning things which they could not see—leading them to believe in His power to forgive sins. . . . John the evangelist says, speaking of the miracles of Christ, "These are written, that ye might believe that Jesus is the Christ, the Son of God; and that believing ye might have life through His name." John 20:31.[164]

Believe

Our part is to pray and believe. Watch unto prayer. Watch, and cooperate with the prayer-hearing God. Bear in mind that "we are laborers together with God." 1 Corinthians 3:9. Speak and act in harmony with your prayers. It will make an infinite difference with you whether trial shall prove your faith to be genuine, or show that your prayers are only a form.[165] If we are willing to do His will, all His strength is ours. Whatever gift He promises, is in the promise itself. "The seed is the Word of God." Luke 8:11. As surely as the oak is in the acorn, so surely is the gift of God in His promise. If we receive the promise, we have the gift.[166] All Heaven is waiting to cooperate with those who will be subordinate to the ways and will of God. God gives grace, and He expects all to use it. He supplies the power if the human mind feels any need or any disposition to receive.... All His biddings are enablings.[167] The gift is in the promise, and we may go about our work assured that what God has promised He is able to perform, and that the gift, which we already possess, will be realized when we need it most.[168]

There are certain conditions upon which we may expect that God will hear and answer our prayers. One of the first of these is that we feel our need of help from Him. He has promised, "I will pour water upon him that is thirsty, and floods upon the dry ground." Isaiah 44:3. Those who hunger and thirst after righteousness, who long after God, may be sure that they will be filled. The heart must be open to the Spirit's influence, or God's blessing cannot be received.[169]

Claim the Promise

Prayer and faith are closely allied, and they need to be studied together. In the prayer of faith there is a divine science; it is a science that everyone who would make his lifework a success must

---

162–*Steps to Christ*, pp. 96, 97.
163–*Steps to Christ*, p. 93.
164–*Steps to Christ*, p. 49.
165–*Christ's Object Lessons*, p. 146.

166–*Education*, p. 253
167–*The Review and Herald*, November 9, 1897.
168–*Education*, p. 258.
169–*Steps to Christ*, p. 95.

understand. Christ says, "What things soever ye desire, when ye pray, believe that ye receive them, and ye shall have them." Mark 11:24. He makes it plain that our asking must be according to God's will; we must ask for the things that He has promised, and whatever we receive must be used in doing His will. The conditions met, the promise is unequivocal.[170] God stands back of every promise He has made. With your Bible in your hands say, I have done as Thou hast said. I present Thy promise, "Ask, and it shall be given you; seek, and ye shall find; knock, and it shall be opened unto you." [Matthew 7:7.][171] "This is the victory that overcometh the world, even our faith." [1 John 5:4.] Prevailing prayer is the prayer of living faith; it takes God at his word, and claims His promises. Feeling has nothing to do with faith.[172] When the soul has been entirely surrendered to God, there will be a firm reliance upon His promises, and earnest prayer and determined effort to control the words and actions.[173]

For the pardon of sin, for the Holy Spirit, for a Christlike temper, for wisdom and strength to do His work, for any gift He has promised, we may ask; then we are to believe that we receive, and return thanks to God that we have received.[174] Earnest, sincere ... prayer would bring strength and grace to resist the powers of darkness. God wants to bless. He is more willing to give the Holy Spirit to them that ask Him than are parents to give good gifts to their children.[175] The same faith which wrought in God's servants of old might work in us. In no less marked a manner than He wrought then will He work now wherever there are hearts of faith to be channels of His power.[176] Prayer and faith will do wonderful things. The Word must be our weapon of warfare. Miracles can be wrought through the Word; for it is profitable for all things.[177]

Prayer is Heaven's ordained means of success in the conflict with sin and the development of Christian character. The divine influences that come in answer to the prayer of faith will accomplish in the soul of the supplicant all for which he pleads.[178] The humble, intelligent prayer of faith, that comes from unfeigned lips, is wholly acceptable to God. It is the heartfelt prayer that is heard in Heaven and rewarded by an answer on Earth. "But to this man will I look, even to him that is poor, and of a contrite spirit, and that trembleth at My word." [Isaiah 66:2.] "For thus saith the High and Lofty One, that inhabiteth eternity, Whose name is Holy; I dwell in the high and holy place, with him also that is of a contrite and a humble spirit, to revive the spirit of the humble, and to revive the heart of the contrite ones." [Isaiah 57:15.] "The sacrifices of God are a broken spirit; a broken and a contrite heart, O God, Thou wilt not despise." [Psalm 51:17.][179] Why should the sons and daughters of God be reluctant to pray, when prayer is the key in the hand of faith to unlock Heaven's store-

---

170–*Education*, pp. 257, 258.
171–*Christ's Object Lessons*, p. 147
172–*The Signs of the Times*, November 18, 1886.
173–*The Review and Herald*, September 1, 1885.
174–*Education*, p. 258.
175–*Our High Calling*, p. 129.
176–*Education*, p. 256.
177–*Evangelism*, p. 489.
178–*The Acts of the Apostles*, p. 564.
179–*The Signs of the Times*, December 3, 1896.

house, where are treasured the boundless resources of Omnipotence?[180]

As Much as You Want

God will be to us everything we will let Him be. Our languid, half-hearted prayers will not bring us returns from Heaven. Oh, we need to press our petitions! Ask in faith, wait in faith, receive in faith, rejoice in hope, for everyone that seeketh findeth. Be in earnest in the matter. Seek God with all the heart. People put soul and earnestness into everything they undertake in temporal things, until their efforts are crowned with success. With intense earnestness learn the trade of seeking the rich blessings that God has promised, and with persevering, determined effort you shall have His light and His truth and His rich grace.[181]

Behold the Son of God bowed in prayer to His Father! Though He is the Son of God, He strengthens His faith by prayer, and by communion with Heaven gathers to Himself power to resist evil and to minister to the needs of men. As the Elder Brother of our race He knows the necessities of those who, compassed with infirmity and living in a world of sin and temptation, still desire to serve Him. He knows that the messengers whom He sees fit to send are weak, erring men; but to all who give themselves wholly to His service He promises divine aid. His Own example is an assurance that earnest, persevering supplication to God in faith—faith that leads to entire dependence upon God, and unreserved consecration to His work—will avail to bring to men the Holy Spirit's aid in the battle against sin.[182]

180–*Christ's Object Lessons*, p. 146.
181–*Our High Calling*, p. 131.

182–*The Acts of the Apostles*, p. 56.

Chapter 7

A Holy Name

Jesus, the divine Master, ever exalted the name of His Heavenly Father. He taught His disciples to pray, "Our Father Who art in Heaven, hallowed be Thy name." Matthew 6:9, A.R.V. And they were not to forget to acknowledge, "Thine is ... the glory." Verse 13. So careful was the Great Healer to direct attention from Himself to the Source of His power, that the wondering multitude, "when they saw the dumb to speak, the maimed to be whole, the lame to walk, and the blind to see," did not glorify Him, but "glorified the God of Israel." Matthew 15:31. In the wonderful prayer that Christ offered just before His crucifixion, He declared, "I have glorified Thee on the Earth." "Glorify Thy Son," He pleaded, "that Thy Son also may glorify Thee." "O righteous Father, the world hath not known Thee: but I have known Thee, and these have known that Thou hast sent Me. And I have declared unto them Thy name, and will declare it: that the love wherewith Thou hast loved Me may be in them, and I in them." John 17:4, 1, 25, 26.

"Thus saith the Lord, Let not the wise man glory in his wisdom, neither let the mighty man glory in his might, let not the rich man glory in his riches: but let him that glorieth glory in this, that he understandeth and knoweth Me, that I am the Lord which exercise loving-kindness, judgment, and righteousness, in the Earth: for in these things I delight, saith the Lord." Jeremiah 9:23, 24.[183]

A Deeper Experience

The sum and substance of the whole matter of Christian grace and experience is comprised in believing on

---

183–*Prophets and Kings*, pp. 69, 70.

Christ,—in knowing God, and his Son, Whom He hath sent. But here is where many fail; for they lack faith in God. Instead of desiring to be brought into fellowship with Christ in His self-denial and humiliation, they are ever seeking for the supremacy of self. As long as they refuse to fall upon the Rock and be broken, they cannot appreciate the love or the character of God. We may be one with Christ; but we must be willing to yield our own way, our own will, and have the mind that was in Christ, that we may know what it is to have fellowship with Him in humiliation and suffering.[184]

"The name of the Lord" is "merciful and gracious, long-suffering, and abundant in goodness and truth, ... forgiving iniquity and transgression and sin." Exodus 34:5–7. Of the church of Christ it is written, "This is the name wherewith she shall be called, The Lord our Righteousness." Jeremiah 33:16. This name is put upon every follower of Christ. It is the heritage of the child of God. The family are called after the Father. The prophet Jeremiah, in the time of Israel's sore distress and tribulation, prayed, "We are called by Thy name; leave us not." Jeremiah 14:9.

A Holy Character

This name is hallowed by the angels of Heaven, by the inhabitants of unfallen worlds. When you pray, "Hallowed be Thy name," you ask that it may be hallowed in this world, hallowed in you. God has acknowledged you before men and angels as His child; pray that you may do no dishonor to the "worthy name by which ye are called." James 2:7. God sends you into the world as His representative. In every act of life you are to make manifest the name of God. This petition calls upon you to possess His character. You cannot hallow His name, you cannot represent Him to the world, unless in life and character you represent the very life and character of God. This you can do only through the acceptance of the grace and righteousness of Christ.[185] It is our privilege to reach higher and still higher for clearer revealings of the character of God.[186] We are called to represent to the world the character of God as it was revealed to Moses…. This is the fruit that God desires from His people. In the purity of their characters, in the holiness of their lives, in their mercy and loving-kindness and compassion, they are to demonstrate that "the law of the Lord is perfect, converting the soul." Psalm 19:7.[187]

[It is by] beholding Christ, by contemplating His character, by learning His lessons, by obeying His words, that we become changed into His likeness.[188] The higher attributes of His being it is our privilege to have, if we will, through the provisions He has made, appropriate these blessings and diligently cultivate the good in the place of the evil. We have reason, conscience, memory, will, affections—all the attributes a human being can possess. Through the provision made when God and the Son of God made a covenant to rescue man from the bondage of Satan, every facility was provided

---

184–*The Bible Echo*, April 15, 1892.

185–*Thoughts From the Mount of Blessing*, pp. 106, 107.
186–*The Ministry of Healing*, p. 464.
187–*Counsels on Health*, pp. 203, 204.
188–*Sabbath-School Worker*, July 1, 1894.

that human nature should come into union with His divine nature.[189]

Worthy of Love

The Lord of life and glory came and dwelt among men. Instead of withdrawing Himself because of the sinfulness of man, instead of confining His labors to a few congenial spirits, and leaving those who knew Him not, to the blindness and ignorance of their sinful hearts, as they deserved to be left, He came nearer to erring humanity. Though in Him dwelt all the fullness of the Godhead bodily, He clothed His divinity with humanity, and established His dwelling place on the Earth, in order that He might demonstrate to men the infinite measure of God's love. He came to reveal to men to what extent the Son of God could submit to humiliation, self-denial, and suffering, in order to accomplish His divine purpose of working out the salvation of men.

The glory of Christ is His character, and it is the character of Christ that draws the hearts of men. Connected with the God of all power, divine sympathy draws minds into harmony with the Divine, and imparts fresh impulses to human hearts. The love of Christ draws the hearts of those who contemplate His humiliation and suffering in the sinner's behalf. They are amazed at the spectacle of God becoming a sacrifice for the guilty, and though they cannot fathom the depths of His love, they submit to be drawn to Him, and respond to His amazing love, exclaiming, "Thy gentleness hath made me great." [2 Samuel 22:36; Psalm 18:35.][190]

The exercise of force is contrary to the principles of God's government; He desires only the service of love; and love cannot be commanded; it cannot be won by force or authority. Only by love is love awakened. To know God is to love Him.[191] God does not force the will or judgment of any. He takes no pleasure in a slavish obedience. He desires that the creatures of His hands shall love Him because He is worthy of love. He would have them obey Him because they have an intelligent appreciation of His wisdom, justice, and benevolence. And all who have a just conception of these qualities will love Him because they are drawn toward Him in admiration of His attributes.[192] When we realize His great love we should be willing to trust everything to the Hand that was nailed to the cross for us.[193]

189–*Selected Messages*, book 3, p. 130.
190–*The Review and Herald*, February 12, 1895.
191–*The Desire of Ages*, p. 22.
192–*The Great Controversy*, p. 541.
193–*Steps to Christ*, p. 103.

Chapter 8

If You Love Me

A love of Jesus is the first result of conversion. The proof of this love is given: "If ye love Me, keep My commandments." "If ye keep My commandments, ye shall abide in My love; even as I have kept My Father's commandments, and abide in His love." [John 14:15; 15:10.][194]

The Greater Love

"There was a certain creditor which had two debtors: the one owed five hundred pence, and the other fifty. And when they had nothing to pay, he frankly forgave them both. Tell Me therefore, which of them will love him most? Simon answered and said, I suppose that he, to whom he forgave most. And He said unto him, Thou hast rightly judged." [Luke 7:41–43.] Jesus takes Simon on his own ground, as feeling himself more righteous than the woman. Then He proceeds to draw the contrast between the love and devotion of the poor penitent, and the unbelief and cold neglect of the self-righteous Jew.

"Seest thou this woman? I entered into thine house, thou gavest Me no water for My feet; but she hath washed My feet with tears, and wiped them with the hairs of her head. Thou gavest Me no kiss; but this woman, since the time I came in, hath not ceased to kiss My feet. My head with oil thou didst not anoint; but this woman hath anointed My feet with ointment. Wherefore I say unto thee, Her sins, which are many, are forgiven; for she loved much. But to whom little is forgiven, the same loveth little." [Verses 44–47.]

Simon had been a great sinner, and also a loathsome leper. Christ had pardoned his sins, and cleansed him from

---
194–*The Signs of the Times*, May 9, 1900.

the terrible disease that was upon him. He had as much cause as the woman he despised, for humility and gratitude to Jesus. But he esteemed himself so highly, he was so intent upon maintaining his own honor and standing, that he was blind to the great debt of gratitude he owed. He had withheld from his Saviour even the acts of courtesy due to a common guest. He did not look upon himself as so great a sinner as he really was. Self-love opened the door to pride, unbelief, and ingratitude. So long as he cherished self-righteousness, he could not place a right estimate upon Christ.[195]

The Cost of Redemption

The plan of salvation is but dimly comprehended by the Christian world. Man, as now taught by men who claim to have a knowledge of the Scriptures, can never know the extent of his fallen, degraded condition; but the mission of Christ will reveal the truth as it is in Jesus. Man can know the depths to which he has sunk only by beholding the wondrous chain of redemption employed to draw him up. The extent of our ruin can be discerned only in the light of the law of God exhibited in the cross of Calvary. The wonderful plan of redemption must be discerned in the death of Christ.[196]

As Christ draws [people] to look upon His cross, to behold Him Whom their sins have pierced, the commandment comes home to the conscience. The wickedness of their life, the deep-seated sin of the soul, is revealed to them. They begin to comprehend something of the righteousness of Christ, and exclaim, "What is sin, that it should require such a sacrifice for the redemption of its victim? Was all this love, all this suffering, all this humiliation, demanded, that we might not perish, but have everlasting life?"

The sinner may resist this love, may refuse to be drawn to Christ; but if he does not resist he will be drawn to Jesus; a knowledge of the plan of salvation will lead him to the foot of the cross in repentance for his sins, which have caused the sufferings of God's dear Son.[197]

Drawn to the Beauty of His Character

The religion that comes from God is the only religion that will lead to God. In order to serve Him aright, we must be born of the divine Spirit. This will purify the heart and renew the mind, giving us a new capacity for knowing and loving God. It will give us a willing obedience to all His requirements. This is true worship. It is the fruit of the working of the Holy Spirit. By the Spirit every sincere prayer is indited, and such prayer is acceptable to God. Wherever a soul reaches out after God, there the Spirit's working is manifest, and God will reveal Himself to that soul. For such worshipers He is seeking. He waits to receive them, and to make them His sons and daughters.[198]

If we would come to Him, let us fix our eyes upon Him; for He is full of grace and truth, and He will let all His goodness pass before us while He hides us in the cleft of the Rock. Then we shall endure as seeing Him Who is invisible, and by

---

195–*The Review and Herald*, March 15, 1887.
196–*The Review and Herald*, February 8, 1898.
197–*Steps to Christ*, p. 27.
198–*The Desire of Ages*, p. 189.

beholding Him, we shall be changed into His image. The reason that we carelessly indulge in sin is that we do not see Jesus. We would not lightly regard sin, did we appreciate the fact that sin wounds our Lord. Did we know Jesus by an experimental knowledge, we would not esteem duty as of small importance; but would manifest faithful integrity in the performance of every service. A right estimate of the character of God would enable us rightly to represent Him to the world. Harshness, roughness in words or manner, evilspeaking, passionate words, cannot exist in the soul that is looking unto Jesus. He who abides in Christ is in an atmosphere that forbids evil, and gives not the slightest excuse for anything of this kind. Spiritual life is not nourished from within, but draws its nutrition from Christ, as the branch does from the vine. We are dependent upon Christ every moment; He is our Source of supply. All our outside forms, prayers, fastings, and almsgiving cannot take the place of the inward work of the Spirit of God on the human heart.

We abide in Christ by faith, by simple childlike trust in His pledged word. Perfect faith, and the surrender of self to God are subjects that should be made very plain to those who are slow to comprehend spiritual things. Faith is not feeling. "Faith is the substance of things hoped for, the evidence of things not seen." [Hebrews 11:1.] The religion that takes the position of secluded enjoyment, that is satisfied to contemplate the religion of Jesus Christ, and that keeps its possessor from an experimental knowledge of its saving power, is a deception.[199]

Love for God

We need to have more of Jesus, and far less of self. We need a childlike simplicity that will lead us to tell the Lord all our wants, and believe that according to His riches and goodness and love He will satisfy our needs. "If ye shall ask anything in My name," He says, "I will do it." [John 14:14.] If you love Me, you will show that love by keeping My commandments. "And I will pray the Father, and He shall give you another Comforter, that He may abide with you forever; even the Spirit of truth. . . ." [Verses 16, 17.]

"He that hath My commandments, and keepeth them, he it is that loveth Me; and he that loveth Me shall be loved of My Father, and I will love him, and will manifest Myself to him." [John 14:21.] This is the only true test of character. In doing the will of God we give the best evidence that we love God and Jesus Christ Whom He has sent. The oft-repeated words of love for God are of no value unless that love is made manifest in the life practice. Love for God is not a mere sentiment; it is a living, working power. The man who does the will of his Father Who is in Heaven shows to the world that he loves God. The fruit of his love is seen in good works.

"If thou shalt confess with thy mouth the Lord Jesus, and shalt believe in thine heart that God hath raised Him from the dead, thou shalt be saved. For with the heart man believeth unto righteousness; and with the mouth confession is made unto salvation." [Romans 10:9, 10.] This means more than an assent to the truth that Christ came into the world and died for the salvation

---

199–*The Youth's Instructor*, February 10, 1898.

of the race. The understanding may be convinced, but the text means more than this. It means entire sincerity. It means faith, intelligent faith, that will cling to the Saviour as the only Hope of a fallen world. It means a faith that will grasp the wonderful provision made, and will engage the affections and control the life, resting upon the merit of a crucified and risen Saviour. It means a faith that works by love and purifies the soul.[200] "If you love Me, let not your love be merely like the supposed feeling of attachment between people. Genuine love lies in the keeping of My commandments." The love that will yield willing obedience is not a fickle thing, but a strong, fixed principle, revealed in word and action.[201]

Thy Will Be Done

"If any man will come after Me," He says, "let him deny himself, and take up his cross, and follow Me." [Matthew 16:24.] Obeying these words, in entire dependence on the Saviour, go forth to give to the world an example of what it means to be a Christian. Yoke up with Christ. This is the only bond of the Gospel. Learn daily how to carry out more acceptable the instruction Christ has given. Live as becomes the subjects of His kingdom. To carry out the words, "Thy will be done on Earth, as it is done in Heaven," [Matthew 6:10]—this is our lifework.[202] In every soul, wherein Christ, the Hope of glory, dwells, are re-echoed the words, "I delight to do Thy will, O my God; yea, Thy law is within my heart. . . ." [Psalm 40:8.] Those who bring their lives into harmony with the prayer that Christ has given will be sanctified through the truth.[203]

The will of God is expressed in the precepts of His holy law, and the principles of this law are the principles of Heaven. The angels of Heaven attain unto no higher knowledge than to know the will of God, and to do His will is the highest service that can engage their powers.[204] The happiness of man is in his obedience to the laws of God. In his obedience to God's law he is surrounded as with a hedge and kept from the evil. No man can be happy and depart from God's specified requirements, and set up a standard of his own which he decides he can safely follow. Then there would be a variety of standards to suit the different minds, and the government taken out of the Lord's hands and human beings grasp the reins of government. The law of self is erected, the will of man is made supreme, and when the high and holy will of God is presented to be obeyed, respected, and honored the human will wants its own way to do its own promptings, and there is a controversy between the human agent and the divine.[205]

They That Keep His Commandments

"Here are they that keep the commandments of God, and the faith of Jesus." [Revelation 14:12.] In order to be prepared for the Judgment, it is necessary that men should keep the law of

---

200–*The Signs of the Times*, May 19, 1898.
201–*Manuscript Releases*, vol. 10, p. 291.
202–*Spalding and Magan Collection*, p. 219.

203–*The Signs of the Times*, October 28, 1903.
204–*Thoughts From the Mount of Blessing*, p. 109.
205–*Manuscript Releases*, vol. 6, p. 338.

God. That law will be the standard of character in the Judgment. The apostle Paul declares: "As many as have sinned in the law shall be judged by the law, ... in the day when God shall judge the secrets of men by Jesus Christ." And he says that "the doers of the law shall be justified." Romans 2:12–16. Faith is essential in order to the keeping of the law of God; for "without faith it is impossible to please Him." And "whatsoever is not of faith is sin." Hebrews 11:6; Romans 14:23.

By the first angel, men are called upon to "fear God, and give glory to Him" and to worship Him as the Creator of the heavens and the Earth. In order to do this, they must obey His law. Says the wise man: "Fear God, and keep His commandments: for this is the whole duty of man." Ecclesiastes 12:13. Without obedience to His commandments no worship can be pleasing to God. "This is the love of God, that we keep His commandments.... 1 John 5:3."[206]

---

[206]–*The Great Controversy*, pp. 435, 436.

Chapter 9

The Water of Death

Death to Self and Sin

Baptism is a most solemn renunciation of the world. Those who are baptized in the threefold name of the Father, the Son, and the Holy Spirit, at the very entrance of their Christian life declare publicly that they have forsaken the service of Satan and have become members of the royal family, children of the heavenly King. They have obeyed the command: "Come out from among them, and be ye separate, ... and touch not the unclean thing." And to them is fulfilled the promise: "I will receive you, and will be a Father unto you, and ye shall be My sons and daughters, saith the Lord Almighty." 2 Corinthians 6:17, 18.[207]

Self must be entirely surrendered.... The Saviour comes very near to those who consecrate themselves to God. If ever there was a time when we needed the working of the Spirit of God upon our hearts and lives, it is now. Let us lay hold of this divine power for strength to live a life of holiness and self-surrender.[208]

Satan does not want anyone to see the necessity of an entire surrender to God. When the soul fails to make this surrender, sin is not forsaken; the appetites and passions are striving for the mastery; temptations confuse the conscience, so that true conversion does not take place.[209] "Except a man be born of water and of the Spirit, he cannot enter into the Kingdom of God...." [John 3:5.] Christ here referred to water baptism and the renewing of the heart by the Spirit of God. ...

"That which is born of the flesh is flesh; and that which is born of the Spirit is spirit." [John 3:6.] By nature the heart is evil, and "who can bring a clean thing out of an unclean? Not one." Job 14:4. No human invention can find a remedy for the sinning soul. "The carnal mind is enmity against God: for it is not subject to the law of God, neither indeed can be." "Out of the heart proceed evil thoughts, murders, adulteries, fornications, thefts, false witness, blasphemies." Romans 8:7; Matthew 15:19. The fountain of the heart must be purified before

---

207–*Testimonies for the Church*, vol. 6, p. 91.
208–*The Review and Herald*, March 3, 1910.

209–*Testimonies for the Church*, vol. 6, p. 92.

the streams can become pure. He who is trying to reach Heaven by his own works in keeping the law is attempting an impossibility. There is no safety for one who has merely a legal religion, a form of godliness. The Christian's life is not a modification or improvement of the old, but a transformation of nature. There is a death to self and sin, and a new life altogether. This change can be brought about only by the effectual working of the Holy Spirit.[210]

The Love of God Toward Man

"After that the kindness and love of God our Saviour toward man appeared, not by works of righteousness which we have done, but according to His mercy He saved us, by the washing of regeneration, and renewing of the Holy Ghost; which He shed on us abundantly through Jesus Christ our Saviour; that being justified by His grace, we should be made heirs according to the hope of eternal life. This is a faithful saying, and these things I will that thou affirm constantly, that they which have believed in God might be careful to maintain good works. These things are good and profitable unto men." Titus 3:4–8. Man was brought again into favor with God by the washing of regeneration. The washing was the burial with Christ in the water in the likeness of His death, representing that all who repent of the transgression of the law of God receive purification, cleansing, through the work of the Holy Spirit. Baptism represents true conversion by the renewing of the Holy Spirit. Those who have been buried with Christ in baptism, and been raised in the likeness of His resurrection, have pledged themselves to live in newness of life.[211]

The Solemn Pledge

By baptism you have taken upon you a solemn pledge. In the name and presence of the Father and the Son and the Holy Ghost, you have solemnly covenanted to be the Lord's. "What shall we say then? Shall we continue in sin, that grace may abound? God forbid. How shall we, that are dead to sin, live any longer therein? Know ye not, that so many of us as were baptized into Jesus Christ were baptized into His death? Therefore we are buried with Him by baptism into death; that like as Christ was raised up from the dead by the glory of the Father, even so we also should walk in newness of life. For if we have been planted together in the likeness of His death, we shall be also in the likeness of His resurrection." [Romans 6:1–5.] I think that if we all understood the sacred ceremony, we should see much more in it than we now discern.

"Let not sin therefore reign in your mortal body, that ye should obey it in the lusts thereof. Neither yield ye your members as instruments of unrighteousness unto sin: but yield yourselves unto God, as those that are alive from the dead, and your members as instruments of righteousness unto God." [Verses 12, 13.] "If ye then be risen with Christ, seek those things which are above, where Christ sitteth on the right hand of God." [Colossians 3:1.][212]

210–*The Desire of Ages*, pp. 171, 172.

211–*The Faith I Live By*, p. 143.
212–*Manuscript Releases*, vol. 6, pp. 25, 26.

"Buried with Him in baptism, wherein also ye are risen with Him through the faith of the operation of God, Who hath raised Him from the dead. And you, being dead in your sins and the uncircumcision of your flesh, hath He quickened together with Him, having forgiven you all trespasses" [Colossians 2:12, 13].

As you openly renounced sin and Satan, the Father, the Son, and the Holy Ghost pledged Themselves to be your sufficiency. As you forsook sin and became dead to the world, you were raised to newness of life by the power which raised Christ from the dead. You came forth from the watery grave, pledged by the solemn covenant of baptism to devote your life to the service of God. You are henceforth to live a new life, as if reason, knowledge, affection, speech, property, had been anew entrusted to you, with a distinct declaration from the Word of God that these gifts are to be recognized as coming from Christ, to be used and improved for Him. You are to take up the life of cross-bearing, cheerfully partaking of the sufferings of Christ. Your life is to be bound up with the life of Christ in obedience to the law of God.

Risen With Christ

"If ye then be risen with Christ, seek those things which are above, where Christ sitteth on the right hand of God. Set your affection on things above, not on things on the Earth. For ye are dead, and your life is hid with Christ in God. When Christ, Who is our life, shall appear, then shall ye also appear with Him in glory." [Colossians 3:1–4]

Jesus, the Son of God, our Sin-Bearer, the Giver of eternal life, speaks to His disciples. Hear what He says: "If any man will come after Me, let him deny himself, and take up his cross, and follow Me." [Matthew 16:24.] He understands every temptation. He can turn the cross into a means of eternal happiness. We must live His life. We must be colaborers with Him. He calls upon His followers to tread in His footsteps of self-denial and self-sacrifice. The character of the Christian is to be a reproduction of Christ. The same love, the same grace, the same unselfish benevolence that characterized the life of the Redeemer is to characterize the lives of His followers.

Let those who have been baptized be true to the vow they have made. "If ye then be risen with Christ, seek those things which are above, where Christ sitteth on the right hand of God" [Colossians 3:1]. You cannot serve God and Mammon. If God be God, follow Him; if Baal, then follow him. No one is compelled to serve God. The full results of a man's choice rest upon himself, for he chooses of his own free will. Let him remember that if he chooses the principles of God, respecting and maintaining them, they become a part of his life, molding him according to the divine similitude. They are in him a well of water, springing up into everlasting life.[213]

None can depend upon their profession of faith as proof that they have a saving connection with Christ. We are not only to say, "I believe," but to practice the truth. It is by conformity to the will of God in our words, our deportment, our character, that we prove our connection with Him. Whenever one renounces

---

213–*Manuscript Releases*, vol. 13, pp. 217–219.

sin, which is the transgression of the law, his life will be brought into conformity to the law, into perfect obedience. This is the work of the Holy Spirit. The light of the Word carefully studied, the voice of conscience, the strivings of the Spirit, produce in the heart genuine love for Christ, Who gave Himself a whole sacrifice to redeem the whole person, body, soul, and spirit. And love is manifested in obedience.[214]

All who share this salvation, purchased for them at such an infinite sacrifice by the Son of God, will follow the example of the true Pattern. Christ was the chief Cornerstone, and we must build upon this Foundation. Each must have a spirit of self-denial and self-sacrifice. The life of Christ upon Earth was unselfish; it was marked with humiliation and sacrifice.... Self-denial is an essential condition of discipleship.[215]

Truth in the Heart

The Holy Spirit first dwells in the heart as the truth, and this He does through the truth. The world, said Christ, cannot receive the Spirit of truth, "because it seeth Him not, neither knoweth Him; but ye know Him; for He dwelleth with you, and shall be in you." [John 14:17.]

"He that hath My commandments, and keepeth them, he it is that loveth Me; and he that loveth Me shall be loved of My Father, and I will love him, and will manifest Myself to him." [Verse 21.] This is the only true test of character. In doing the will of God we give the best evidence that we love God and Jesus Christ Whom He has sent. The oft-repeated words of love for God are of no value unless that love is made manifest in the life practice. Love for God is not a mere sentiment; it is a living, working power. The man who does the will of his Father Who is in Heaven shows to the world that he loves God. The fruit of his love is seen in good works.

"If thou shalt confess with thy mouth the Lord Jesus, and shalt believe in thine heart that God hath raised Him from the dead, thou shalt be saved. For with the heart man believeth unto righteousness; and with the mouth confession is made unto salvation." [Romans 10:9, 10.] This means more than an assent to the truth that Christ came into the world and died for the salvation of the race. The understanding may be convinced, but the text means more than this. It means entire sincerity. It means faith, intelligent faith, that will cling to the Saviour as the only Hope of a fallen world. It means a faith that will grasp the wonderful provision made, and will engage the affections and control the life, resting upon the merit of a crucified and risen Saviour. It means a faith that works by love and purifies the soul.[216]

214–*Testimonies for the Church*, vol. 6, p. 91.
215–*Testimonies for the Church*, vol. 3, pp. 387, 388.

216–*The Signs of the Times*, May 19, 1898.

Abundant Life

He who is made complete in Christ must first be emptied of pride, of self-sufficiency. Then there is silence in the soul, and God's voice can be heard. Then the Spirit can find unobstructed entrance. Let God work in and through you. Then with Paul you can say, "I live; yet not I but Christ liveth in me." [Galatians 2:20.] But until self is laid on the altar, until we let the Holy Spirit mould and fashion us according to the divine similitude, we cannot reach God's ideal for us.

Christ said, "I am come that they might have life, and that they might have it more abundantly." [John 10:10.] This life is what we must have in order to work for Christ, and we must have it "more abundantly." God will breathe this life into every soul that dies to self. But entire self-renunciation is required. Unless this takes place, we carry with us that which destroys our happiness and usefulness.

The Lord needs men and women who carry with them into the daily life the light of a godly example, men and women whose words and actions show that Christ is abiding in the heart, teaching, leading, and guiding. He needs men and women of prayer, who, by wrestling alone with God, obtain the victory over self, and then go forth to impart to others that which they have received from the Source of power. God accepts those who crucify self, and makes them vessels unto honor. They are in His hands as clay in the hands of the potter, and He works His will through them. Such men and women receive spiritual power. Christ lives in them, and the power of His Spirit attends their efforts. They realize that they are to live in this world the life that Jesus lived,—a life free from all selfishness; and He enables them to bear witness for Him that draws souls to the cross of Calvary.[217]

217–*The Signs of the Times*, April 9, 1902.

Chapter 10

The Will

In the Heart

The perception and appreciation of truth ... depends less upon the mind than upon the heart. Truth must be received into the soul; it claims the homage of the will. If truth could be submitted to the reason alone, pride would be no hindrance in the way of its reception. But it is to be received through the work of grace in the heart; and its reception depends upon the renunciation of every sin that the Spirit of God reveals. Man's advantages for obtaining a knowledge of the truth, however great these may be, will prove of no benefit to him unless the heart is open to receive the truth, and there is a conscientious surrender of every habit and practice that is opposed to its principles. To those who thus yield themselves to God, having an honest desire to know and to do His will, the truth is revealed as the power of God for their salvation. These will be able to distinguish between him who speaks for God, and him who speaks merely from himself. The Pharisees had not put their will on the side of God's will. They were not seeking to know the truth, but to find some excuse for evading it; Christ showed that this was why they did not understand His teaching.[218]

The Greatest Battle

There are but two powers that control the minds of men—the power of God and the power of Satan.[219] The warfare against self is the greatest battle that was ever fought. The yielding of self, surrendering all to the will of God, requires a struggle; but the soul must submit to God before it can be renewed in holiness.[220]

You need to drink daily at the fountain of truth, that you may understand the secret of pleasure and joy in the Lord.

218–*The Desire of Ages*, pp. 455, 456.
219–*Temperance*, p. 276.
220–*Steps to Christ*, p. 43.

But you must remember that your will is the spring of all your actions. This will, that forms so important a factor in the character of man, was at the Fall given into the control of Satan; and he has ever since been working in man to will and to do of his own pleasure, but to the utter ruin and misery of man.[221] An impure thought tolerated, an unholy desire cherished, and the soul is contaminated, its integrity compromised. "Then when lust hath conceived, it bringeth forth sin: and sin, when it is finished, bringeth forth death." [James 1:15.] If we would not commit sin, we must shun its very beginnings. Every emotion and desire must be held in subjection to reason and conscience. Every unholy thought must be instantly repelled. To your closet, followers of Christ. Pray in faith and with all the heart. Satan is watching to ensnare your feet. You must have help from above if you would escape his devices.[222]

You desire to give yourself to Him, but you are weak in moral power, in slavery to doubt, and controlled by the habits of your life of sin. Your promises and resolutions are like ropes of sand. You cannot control your thoughts, your impulses, your affections. The knowledge of your broken promises and forfeited pledges weakens your confidence in your own sincerity, and causes you to feel that God cannot accept you; but you need not despair. What you need to understand is the true force of the will. This is the governing power in the nature of man, the power of decision, or of choice. Everything depends on the right action of the will. The power of choice God has given to men; it is theirs to exercise. You cannot change your heart, you cannot of yourself give to God its affections; but you can choose to serve Him. You can give Him your will.[223] The infinite sacrifice of God in giving Jesus, His beloved Son, to become a Sacrifice for sin, enables Him to say, without violating one principle of His government: "Yield yourself up to Me; give Me that will; take it from the control of Satan, and I will take possession of it; then I can work in you to will and to do of My good pleasure." When He gives you the mind of Christ, your will becomes as His will, and your character is transformed to be like Christ's character.[224]

Reasoning Together

Our will is not to be forced into cooperation with divine agencies, but it must be voluntarily submitted.[225] The Lord does not sanction in any one of us a blind, stupid credulity. He does not dishonor the human understanding, but, far from this, He calls for the human will to be brought into connection with the divine will. He calls for the ingenuity of the human mind, the tact, the skill, to be strenuously exercised in searching out the truth *as it is in Jesus*.... Ye are laborers together with God.[226]

[Jesus] shows by His willing obedience that man may keep the law of God and that transgression of the law, not obedience to it, brings him into bondage. The Saviour was full of compassion and

---

221–*Testimonies for the Church*, vol. 5, p. 515.
222–*Testimonies for the Church*, vol. 5, p. 177.
223–*Steps to Christ*, p. 47.
224–*Testimonies for the Church*, vol. 5, p. 515.
225–*Thoughts From the Mount of Blessing*, p. 142.
226–*Our High Calling*, p. 310.

love; He never spurned the truly penitent, however great their guilt; but He severely denounced hypocrisy of every sort. He is acquainted with the sins of men, He knows all their acts and reads their secret motives; yet He does not turn away from them in their iniquity. He pleads and reasons with the sinner, and in one sense—that of having Himself borne the weakness of humanity—He puts Himself on a level with him. "Come now, and let us reason together, saith the Lord: though your sins be as scarlet, they shall be as white as snow; though they be red like crimson, they shall be as wool." [Isaiah 1:18.][227]

How to Believe

From the simple Bible account of how Jesus healed the sick, we may learn something about how to believe in Him for the forgiveness of sins. Let us turn to the story of the paralytic at Bethesda. The poor sufferer was helpless; he had not used his limbs for thirty-eight years. Yet Jesus bade him, "Rise, take up thy bed, and walk." [John 5:8.] The sick man might have said, "Lord, if Thou wilt make me whole, I will obey Thy word." But, no, he believed Christ's word, believed that he was made whole, and he made the effort at once; he willed to walk, and he did walk. He acted on the word of Christ, and God gave the power. He was made whole.

In like manner you are a sinner. You cannot atone for your past sins; you cannot change your heart and make yourself holy. But God promises to do all this for you through Christ. You believe that promise. You confess your sins and give yourself to God. You will to serve Him. Just as surely as you do this, God will fulfill His word to you. If you believe the promise—believe that you are forgiven and cleansed—God supplies the fact; you are made whole, just as Christ gave the paralytic power to walk when the man believed that he was healed. It is so if you believe it.[228] Where there is not only a belief in God's Word, but a submission of the will to Him; where the heart is yielded to Him, the affections fixed upon Him, there is faith—faith that works by love and purifies the soul. Through this faith the heart is renewed in the image of God.[229]

Expulsion

Faith works by love, and purifies the soul, expelling the love of sin that leads to rebellion against, and transgression of, the law of God. This true love in the heart always leads its possessor into harmony with the commandments of God; for through the agency of the Holy Spirit, the character is transformed, and the mind and will of the human agent are brought into perfect conformity to the divine will, and this is conformity to the divine standard of righteousness.[230]

Paul wrote to [his] brethren as "saints in Christ Jesus;" [Philippians 1:1] but he was not writing to those who were perfect in character. He wrote to them as men and women who were striving against temptation and who were in danger of falling. He pointed them to "the God of peace, that brought again from the dead our Lord Jesus, that Great

---

227–*Testimonies for the Church*, vol. 4, p. 294.

228–*Steps to Christ*, pp. 50, 51.
229–*Steps to Christ*, p. 63.
230–*The Youth's Instructor*, February 17, 1898.

Shepherd of the sheep." He assured them that "through the blood of the everlasting covenant" He will "make you perfect in every good work to do His will, working in you that which is well pleasing in His sight, through Jesus Christ." Hebrews 13:20, 21.[231]

Wholehearted

Christ is the Source of every right impulse. He is the only One that can implant in the heart enmity against sin. Every desire for truth and purity, every conviction of our own sinfulness, is an evidence that His Spirit is moving upon our hearts.[232] If man places his will on God's side, fully surrendering self to God's will, the high and holy endeavor of the human agent takes down the obstruction he himself has erected, the rubbish is cleared away from the door of the heart, the defiance barricading the soul is broken down. The door of the heart is opened and Jesus enters, to abide as a welcome Guest.[233] Thus your whole nature will be brought under the control of the Spirit of Christ; your affections will be centered upon Him, your thoughts will be in harmony with Him.[234] The whole mind, the whole soul, the whole heart, and the whole strength are purchased by the blood of the Son of God.... If our hearts are united with Christ's heart, we shall have a most intense desire to be clothed with His righteousness.[235]

You are to maintain this connection with Christ by faith and the continual surrender of your will to Him; and so long as you do this, He will work in you to will and to do according to His good pleasure. So you may say, "The life which I now live in the flesh I live by the faith of the Son of God, Who loved me, and gave Himself for me." Galatians 2:20.... Then with Christ working in you, you will manifest the same spirit and do the same works,—works of righteousness, obedience.[236]

God expects those who bear the name of Christ to represent Him in thought, word, and deed. Their thoughts are to be pure, and their words and deeds noble and uplifting, drawing those around them nearer to the Saviour. In the life of the true Christian there is nothing of self. Self is dead. There was no selfishness in the life that Christ lived while on this Earth. Bearing our nature, He lived a life wholly devoted to the service of others.[237]

God's Word sets forth the will that is to be carried into the recesses of the soul.[238] All true obedience comes from the heart. It was heart work with Christ. And if we consent, He will so identify Himself with our thoughts and aims, so blend our hearts and minds into conformity to His will, that when obeying Him we shall be but carrying out our own impulses. The will, refined and sanctified, will find its highest delight in doing His service. When we know God as it is our privilege to know Him, our life will be a life of continual obedience. Through an appreciation of the character of Christ, through communion with God, sin will

---

231–*The Ministry of Healing*, p. 167.
232–*Steps to Christ*, p. 26.
233–*In Heavenly Places*, p. 27.
234–*Steps to Christ*, p. 47.
235–*Testimonies to Ministers and Gospel Workers*, pp. 130, 131.

236–*Steps to Christ*, pp. 62, 63.
237–*The Review and Herald*, November 23, 1905.
238–*Manuscript Releases*, vol. 10, p. 295.

become hateful to us.[239]

As Jesus rested by faith in the Father's care, so we are to rest in the care of our Saviour. If the disciples had trusted in Him, they would have been kept in peace. Their fear in the time of danger revealed their unbelief. In their efforts to save themselves, they forgot Jesus; and it was only when, in despair of self-dependence, they turned to Him that He could give them help.

How often the disciples' experience is ours! When the tempests of temptation gather, and the fierce lightnings flash, and the waves sweep over us, we battle with the storm alone, forgetting that there is One Who can help us. We trust to our own strength till our hope is lost, and we are ready to perish. Then we remember Jesus, and if we call upon Him to save us, we shall not cry in vain. Though He sorrowfully reproves our unbelief and self-confidence, He never fails to give us the help we need. Whether on the land or on the sea, if we have the Saviour in our hearts, there is no need of fear. Living faith in the Redeemer will smooth the sea of life, and will deliver us from danger in the way that He knows to be best.[240]

Lord, Lord

In the Sermon on the Mount Christ said, "Not everyone that saith unto Me, Lord, Lord, shall enter into the Kingdom of Heaven; but he that doeth the will of My Father Which is in Heaven." Matthew 7:21. The test of sincerity is not in words, but in deeds. Christ does not say to any man, What say ye more than others? but, "What do ye more than others?" Matthew 5:47. Full of meaning are His words, "If ye know these things, happy are ye if ye do them." John 13:17. Words are of no value unless they are accompanied with appropriate deeds.[241]

Genuine faith will lead men to work out their own salvation with fear and trembling. They will not follow the course of this world. The Spirit and works of Christ will be manifested in their lives and the Word of God will be made the rule of their action. They will do and teach the commandments of God, and will walk humbly before men and angels. They will discern the work of God in the Earth, and prejudice will not be permitted to close their hearts against the truth for their time. They will strive to enter in at the strait gate, they will take the narrow way and follow the Redeemer of the world.[242]

God has given us His holy precepts, because He loves mankind. To shield us from the results of transgression, He reveals the principles of righteousness. The law is an expression of the thought of God; when received in Christ, it becomes our thought. It lifts us above the power of natural desires and tendencies, above temptations that lead to sin. God desires us to be happy, and He gave us the precepts of the law that in obeying them we might have joy.[243]

"My meat is to do the will of Him that sent Me, and to accomplish His work." John 4:34, R.V. As His words to the woman had aroused her conscience, Jesus rejoiced. He saw her drinking of the water of life, and His Own hunger and

---

239–*The Desire of Ages*, p. 668.
240–*The Desire of Ages*, p. 336.
241–*Christ's Object Lessons*, p. 272.
242–*The Signs of the Times*, March 30, 1888.
243–*The Desire of Ages*, p. 308.

thirst were satisfied. The accomplishment of the mission which He had left Heaven to perform strengthened the Saviour for His labor, and lifted Him above the necessities of humanity. To minister to a soul hungering and thirsting for the truth was more grateful to Him than eating or drinking. It was a comfort, a refreshment, to Him. Benevolence was the life of His soul.[244] He said, "The Son of Man came not to be ministered unto, but to minister, and to give His life a ransom for many." Matthew 20:28. This was the one great object of His life. Everything else was secondary and subservient. It was His meat and drink to do the will of God and to finish His work. Self and self-interest had no part in His labor.[245]

God stands toward His people in the relation of a Father, and He has a Father's claim to our faithful service. Consider the life of Christ. Standing at the head of humanity, serving His Father, He is an example of what every son should and may be. The obedience that Christ rendered God requires from human beings today. He served His Father with love, in willingness and freedom. "I delight to do Thy will, O My God," He declared; "yea, Thy law is within My heart." Psalm 40:8. Christ counted no sacrifice too great, no toil too hard, in order to accomplish the work which He came to do.[246]

The yoke that binds to service is the law of God. The great law of love revealed in Eden, proclaimed upon Sinai, and in the new covenant written in the heart, is that which binds the human worker to the will of God. If we were left to follow our own inclinations, to go just where our will would lead us, we should fall into Satan's ranks and become possessors of his attributes. Therefore God confines us to His will, which is high, and noble, and elevating. He desires that we shall patiently and wisely take up the duties of service. The yoke of service Christ Himself has borne in humanity. He said, "I delight to do Thy will, O My God: yea, Thy law is within My heart." Psalm 40:8. "I came down from Heaven, not to do Mine Own will, but the will of Him that sent Me." John 6:38. Love for God, zeal for His glory, and love for fallen humanity, brought Jesus to Earth to suffer and to die. This was the controlling power of His life. This principle He bids us adopt.[247]

The loveliness of the character of Christ will be seen in His followers. It was His delight to do the will of God.[248] If we abide in Christ, if the love of God dwells in us, our feelings, our thoughts, our purposes, our actions, will be in harmony with the will of God as expressed in the precepts of His holy law.[249]

Believe on Him

"What shall we do, that we might work the works of God?" [John 6:28.] They had been performing many and burdensome works in order to recommend themselves to God; and they were ready to hear of any new observance by which they could secure greater merit. Their question meant, What shall we do

---

244–*The Desire of Ages*, pp. 190, 191.
245–*Steps to Christ*, p. 78.
246–*Christ's Object Lessons*, p. 282.

247–*The Desire of Ages*, pp. 329, 330.
248–*Steps to Christ*, p. 59.
249–*Steps to Christ*, p. 61.

that we may deserve Heaven? What is the price we are required to pay in order to obtain the life to come?

"Jesus answered and said unto them, This is the work of God, that ye believe on Him Whom He hath sent." [John 6:29.] The price of Heaven is Jesus. The way to Heaven is through faith in "the Lamb of God, Which taketh away the sin of the world." John 1:29.[250]

What Christ works within, will be worked out under the dictation of a converted intellect. The plan of beginning outside and trying to work inward has always failed, and always will fail. God's plan with you is to begin at the very seat of all difficulties, the heart, and then from out of the heart will issue the principles of righteousness; the reformation will be outward as well as inward.[251] As the leaven, when mingled with the meal, works from within outward, so it is by the renewing of the heart that the grace of God works to transform the life. No mere external change is sufficient to bring us into harmony with God. There are many who try to reform by correcting this or that bad habit, and they hope in this way to become Christians, but they are beginning in the wrong place. Our first work is with the heart.[252]

Abide in Him

The soul that abides in Christ can never be barren nor unfruitful. You must draw your supplies from Him Who is the Source of all strength and sufficiency. If you will abide in Christ, He will be with you, and will bestow upon you every gift necessary for your success in this work. In your lack of confidence in yourself, look unto Jesus. Look and live; for in Him are life and light. Lean on God. He will supply all your needs; He will be made unto you wisdom, and righteousness, and sanctification, and redemption. As the human agent contemplates the character of Christ, and abides in His love, the mind of Christ is transferred to him, and he bears the image of the Divine. Thus it was with Moses and Stephen. Christ was in them, and was revealed in their daily life.

We are nearing the close of this Earth's history; soon we shall stand before the great white throne. Your opportunities for work will soon be past. Therefore work while it is called today. With the help of God, every true believer can see where there is work to be done. When the human will cooperates with the will of God, it becomes omnipotent.[253]

"I will establish My covenant with thee, and thou shalt know that I am the Lord; that thou mayest remember, and be confounded, and never open thy mouth anymore because of thy shame, when I am pacified toward thee for all that thou hast done, saith the Lord God." Ezekiel 16:62, 63. Then our lips will not be opened in self-glorification. We shall know that our sufficiency is in

---

250–*The Desire of Ages*, p. 385.
251–*Manuscript Releases*, vol. 20, p. 112.
252–*Christ's Object Lessons*, p. 97.

253–*The Youth's Instructor*, June 24, 1897.

The Will

Christ alone. We shall make the apostle's confession our own. "I know that in me (that is, in my flesh) dwelleth no good thing." Romans 7:18. "God forbid that I should glory, save in the cross of our Lord Jesus Christ, by Whom the world is crucified unto me, and I unto the world." Galatians 6:14.

In harmony with this experience is the command, "Work out your own salvation with fear and trembling. For it is God Which worketh in you both to will and to do of His good pleasure." Philippians 2:12, 13. God does not bid you fear that He will fail to fulfill His promises, that His patience will weary, or His compassion be found wanting. Fear lest your will shall not be held in subjection to Christ's will, lest your hereditary and cultivated traits of character shall control your life. "It is God Which worketh in you both to will and to do of His good pleasure." Fear lest self shall interpose between your soul and the great Master Worker. Fear lest self-will shall mar the high purpose that through you God desires to accomplish. Fear to trust to your own strength, fear to withdraw your hand from the hand of Christ and attempt to walk life's pathway without His abiding presence.[254]

---

[254]–*Christ's Object Lessons*, p. 161.

Chapter 11

Forgiveness

That which should cause us the deepest joy is the fact that God forgives sin. If we take Him at His word and forsake our sins, He is ready and willing to cleanse us from all unrighteousness. He will give us a pure heart and the abiding presence of His Spirit, for Jesus lives to intercede for us. But ... spiritual things are spiritually discerned. It is a living, active, abiding faith that discerns the will of God, that appropriates the promises, and profits by the truths of His Word.[255]

Repentance as well as forgiveness is the gift of God through Christ. It is through the influence of the Holy Spirit that we are convinced of sin, and feel our need of pardon. None but the contrite are forgiven; but it is the grace of the Lord that makes the heart penitent. He is acquainted with all our weaknesses and infirmities, and He will help us. He will hear the prayer of faith; but the sincerity of prayer can be proved only by our efforts to bring ourselves into harmony with the great moral standard which will test every man's character. We need to open our hearts to the influence of the Spirit, and to experience its transforming power.[256]

As We Forgive

Jesus teaches that we can receive forgiveness from God only as we forgive others. It is the love of God that draws us unto Him, and that love cannot touch our hearts without creating love for our brethren.

After completing the Lord's Prayer, Jesus added: "If ye forgive men their trespasses, your Heavenly Father will also forgive you: but if ye forgive not men their trespasses, neither will

---

255–*In Heavenly Places*, p. 348.

256–*The Review and Herald*, June 24, 1884.

your Father forgive your trespasses." [Matthew 6:14, 15.] He who is unforgiving cuts off the very channel through which alone he can receive mercy from God. We should not think that unless those who have injured us confess the wrong we are justified in withholding from them our forgiveness.[257] We should not accumulate our grievances, holding them to our hearts until the one we think guilty has humbled his heart by repentance and confession. This is his part no doubt, and the thing he must do in order to clear his soul from the sin he has committed. But with him we have nothing to do in this matter, and should only seek to stand before God in the way He would have us, that our prayers be not hindered. We are to have a spirit of pity, of compassion toward those who have trespassed against us, whether or not they confess their faults. If they fail to repent and make confession, their sins will stand registered in the books above to confront them in the day of Judgment; but if they say, "I repent," then our duty is plain; we are freely to forgive from the heart their trespasses against us as we hope to be forgiven by our Heavenly Father. However sorely they may have wounded us, we are not to cherish our grievances and sympathize with ourselves over our injuries, but as we hope to be pardoned for our offenses against God, so must we pardon those who have done evil to us.[258]

When we come to ask mercy and blessing from God we should have a spirit of love and forgiveness in our own hearts. How can we pray, "Forgive us our debts, as we forgive our debtors," and yet indulge an unforgiving spirit? Matthew 6:12. If we expect our own prayers to be heard we must forgive others in the same manner and to the same extent as we hope to be forgiven.[259]

One of the most common sins, and one that is attended with most pernicious results, is the indulgence of an unforgiving spirit. How many will cherish animosity or revenge, and then bow before God and ask to be forgiven as they forgive.[260] But few realize the true import of this prayer. If those who are unforgiving did comprehend the depth of its meaning they would not dare to repeat it and ask God to deal with them as they deal with their fellow mortals. And yet this spirit of hardness and lack of forgiveness exists even among brethren to a fearful extent.[261] Many who have stood in high places as Christians upon Earth, will not be found with the happy throng that shall surround the throne. Those who have had knowledge and talent, and yet have delighted in controversy and unholy strife, will not have a place with the redeemed.[262]

A Heart Ruled by Love

The heart in which love rules, will not be filled with passion or revenge, by injuries which pride and self-love would deem unbearable. Love is unsuspecting, ever placing the most favorable construction upon the motives and acts

---

257–*Thoughts From the Mount of Blessing*, pp. 113, 114.
258–*The Youth's Instructor*, June 1, 1893.
259–*Steps to Christ*, p. 97.
260–*The Signs of the Times*, February 1, 1883.
261–*Testimonies for the Church*, vol. 3, p. 95.
262–*The Signs of the Times*, February 24, 1890.

of others. Love will never needlessly expose the faults of others.[263]

Pure love thinketh no evil. When we constantly imagine that we are not appreciated, and watch for slights, we do ourselves and others great harm. We must forget self in loving service for others.[264] But especially we should manifest compassion and respect for those who are giving their lives to the cause of God.... It takes special watchfulness to keep the affections alive, and our hearts in a condition where we shall be sensible of the good that exists in the hearts of others. If we do not watch on this point, Satan will put his jealousy into our souls; he will put his glasses before our eyes, that we may see the actions of our brethren in a distorted light. Instead of looking critically upon our brethren, we should turn our eyes within, and be ready to discover the objectionable traits of our own character. As we have a proper realization of our own mistakes and failures, the mistakes of others will sink into insignificance.[265]

Evilspeaking

We cannot afford to live on the husks of others' faults or failings. Evilspeaking is a twofold curse, falling more heavily upon the speaker than upon the hearer. He who scatters the seeds of dissension and strife reaps in his own soul the deadly fruits. The very act of looking for evil in others develops evil in those who look. By dwelling upon the faults of others, we are changed into the same image. But by beholding Jesus, talking of His love and perfection of character, we become changed into His image. By contemplating the lofty ideal He has placed before us, we shall be uplifted into a pure and holy atmosphere, even the presence of God. When we abide here, there goes forth from us a light that irradiates all who are connected with us.

Instead of criticizing and condemning others, say, "I must work out my own salvation. If I cooperate with Him Who desires to save my soul, I must watch myself diligently. I must put away every evil from my life. I must overcome every fault. I must become a new creature in Christ. Then, instead of weakening those who are striving against evil, I can strengthen them by encouraging words." We are too indifferent in regard to one another. Too often we forget that our fellow laborers are in need of strength and cheer. Take care to assure them of your interest and sympathy. Help them by your prayers, and let them know that you do it.[266]

We are dependent upon the pardoning mercy of God every day and every hour; how then can we cherish bitterness and malice toward our fellow sinners! If, in all their daily intercourse, Christians would carry out the principles of this prayer, what a blessed change would be wrought in the church and in the world! This would be the most convincing testimony that could be given to the reality of Bible religion.[267] If Christ is taken as our Pattern in all things, if He is formed within, "the Hope of glory" [Colossians 1:27], our minds will be filled with thoughts that are pure and lovely.

263–*The Signs of the Times*, February 1, 1883.
264–*The Signs of the Times*, February 1, 1883.
265–*The Review and Herald*, February 24, 1891.

266–*The Ministry of Healing*, pp. 492, 493.
267–*The Signs of the Times*, February 1, 1883.

We shall feel no inclination to think or to talk of the failings of others, or to triumph over the knowledge of a brother's error. Mercy and love will be cherished; that charity which "suffereth long and is kind," which "beareth all things" and "thinketh no evil," will appear in word and action. [1 Corinthians 13:4, 7, 5.][268]

Seek to Save

"If thy brother shall trespass against thee," Christ said, "go and tell him his fault between thee and him alone: if he shall hear thee, thou hast gained thy brother. But if he will not hear thee, then take with thee one or two more, that in the mouth of two or three witnesses every word may be established. And if he shall neglect to hear them, tell it unto the church: but if he neglect to hear the church, let him be unto thee as an heathen man and a publican." Matthew 18:15–17.

Our Lord teaches that matters of difficulty between Christians are to be settled within the church. They should not be opened before those who do not fear God. If a Christian is wronged by his brother, let him not appeal to unbelievers in a court of justice. Let him follow out the instruction Christ has given. Instead of trying to avenge himself, let him seek to save his brother. God will guard the interests of those who love and fear Him, and with confidence we may commit our case to Him Who judges righteously.

Too often when wrongs are committed again and again, and the wrongdoer confesses his fault, the injured one becomes weary, and thinks he has forgiven quite enough. But the Saviour has plainly told us how to deal with the erring: "If thy brother trespass against thee, rebuke him; and if he repent, forgive him." Luke 17:3. Do not hold him off as unworthy of your confidence. Consider "thyself, lest thou also be tempted." Galatians 6:1.

If your brethren err, you are to forgive them. When they come to you with confession, you should not say, I do not think they are humble enough. I do not think they feel their confession. What right have you to judge them, as if you could read the heart? The Word of God says, "If he repent, forgive him. And if he trespasses against thee seven times in a day, and seven times in a day turn again to thee, saying, I repent; thou shalt forgive him." Luke 17:3, 4. And not only seven times, but seventy times seven—just as often as God forgives you.

Grace That Is Greater

We ourselves owe everything to God's free grace. Grace in the covenant ordained our adoption. Grace in the Saviour effected our redemption, our regeneration, and our exaltation to heirship with Christ. Let this grace be revealed to others.

Give the erring one no occasion for discouragement. Suffer not a Pharisaical hardness to come in and hurt your brother. Let no bitter sneer rise in mind or heart. Let no tinge of scorn be manifest in the voice. If you speak a word of your own, if you take an attitude of indifference, or show suspicion or distrust, it may prove the ruin of a soul. He needs a brother with the Elder Brother's heart of sympathy to touch his heart of humanity. Let him feel

---

268–*The Review and Herald*, February 16, 1897.

the strong clasp of a sympathizing hand, and hear the whisper, "Let us pray." God will give a rich experience to you both. Prayer unites us with one another and with God. Prayer brings Jesus to our side, and gives to the fainting, perplexed soul new strength to overcome the world, the flesh, and the Devil. Prayer turns aside the attacks of Satan.

When one turns away from human imperfections to behold Jesus, a divine transformation takes place in the character. The Spirit of Christ working upon the heart conforms it to His image. Then let it be your effort to lift up Jesus. Let the mind's eye be directed to "the Lamb of God, Which taketh away the sin of the world." John 1:29. And as you engage in this work, remember that "he which converteth the sinner from the error of his way, shall save a soul from death, and shall hide a multitude of sins." James 5:20.

"But if ye forgive not men their trespasses, neither will your Father forgive your trespasses." Matthew 6:15. Nothing can justify an unforgiving spirit. He who is unmerciful toward others shows that he himself is not a partaker of God's pardoning grace. In God's forgiveness the heart of the erring one is drawn close to the great heart of Infinite Love. The tide of divine compassion flows into the sinner's soul, and from him to the souls of others. The tenderness and mercy that Christ has revealed in His Own precious life will be seen in those who become sharers of His grace. But "if any man have not the Spirit of Christ, he is none of His." Romans 8:9. He is alienated from God, fitted only for eternal separation from Him.

It is true that he may once have received forgiveness; but his unmerciful spirit shows that he now rejects God's pardoning love. He has separated himself from God, and is in the same condition as before he was forgiven. He has denied his repentance, and his sins are upon him as if he had not repented.

But the great lesson of the parable [of the unmerciful debtor] lies in the contrast between God's compassion and man's hardheartedness; in the fact that God's forgiving mercy is to be the measure of our own. "Shouldest not thou also have had compassion on thy fellow servant, even as I had pity on thee?" [Matthew 18:33.]

We are not forgiven *because* we forgive, but *as* we forgive. The ground of all forgiveness is found in the unmerited love of God, but by our attitude toward others we show whether we have made that love our own. Wherefore Christ says, "With what judgment ye judge, ye shall be judged; and with what measure ye mete, it shall be measured to you again." Matthew 7:2.[269]

269–*Christ's Object Lessons*, pp. 248–251.

Chapter 12

The Only Way

Colaborers With Christ

In the plan of restoring in men the divine image, it was provided that the Holy Spirit should move upon human minds, and be as the presence of Christ, a molding agency upon human character. Receiving the truth, men become also recipients of the grace of Christ, and devote their sanctified human ability to the work in which Christ was engaged,—men become laborers together with God. It is to make men agents for God, that divine truth is brought home to their understanding.[270] God is the Source of life and light and joy to the universe. Like rays of light from the sun, like the streams of water bursting from a living spring, blessings flow out from Him to all His creatures. And wherever the life of God is in the hearts of men, it will flow out to others in love and blessing.[271]

It is because of the Lord's mercy that men are permitted to have a part in the work of salvation, and be colaborers together with Christ, in caring for the souls for whom He died. It is by engaging in this work that we are enabled to grow in grace and in the knowledge of the Lord Jesus Christ.[272] Love to Jesus will be manifested in a desire to work as He worked for the blessing and uplifting of humanity. It will lead to love, tenderness, and sympathy toward all the creatures of our Heavenly Father's care.[273]

The spirit of unselfish labor for others gives depth, stability, and Christlike loveliness to the character, and brings peace and happiness to its possessor. The aspirations are elevated. There is no room for sloth or selfishness. Those who thus exercise the Christian graces will grow and will become strong to work for God. They are most surely working out their own salvation.[274]

270–*The Review and Herald*, February 12, 1895.
271–*Steps to Christ*, p. 77.
272–*General Conference Bulletin*, October 1, 1896.
273–*Steps to Christ*, pp. 77, 78.
274–*The Signs of the Times*, March 19, 1902.

The apostle says of those who profess to serve Jesus, "Ye are laborers together with God." [1 Corinthians 3:9.] All our ability, all our talents, are to be brought into working order in union with divine agencies, or we shall never be overcomers, and inherit eternal life. Self must die. Every practice, every habit, that has a harmful tendency, however innocent it may be regarded by the world, must be battled with until overcome, that the human agent may perfect a character after the divine Pattern. The apostle says: "Work out your own salvation with fear and trembling. For it is God that worketh in you both to will and to do of His good pleasure. Do all things without murmurings and disputings; that ye may be blameless and harmless [you must be blameless in order to be harmless], the sons of God, without rebuke, in the midst of a crooked and perverse nation, among whom ye shine as lights in the world; holding forth the Word of life; that I may rejoice in the day of Christ, that I have not run in vain, neither labored in vain." [Philippians 2:12–16.][275]

Our Saviour's joy was in the uplifting and redemption of fallen men. For this He counted not His life dear unto Himself, but endured the cross, despising the shame. So angels are ever engaged in working for the happiness of others. This is their joy. That which selfish hearts would regard as humiliating service, ministering to those who are wretched and in every way inferior in character and rank, is the work of sinless angels. The spirit of Christ's self-sacrificing love is the spirit that pervades Heaven and is the very essence of its bliss. This is the spirit that Christ's followers will possess, the work that they will do.[276]

The Duty at Hand

Christ's method alone will give true success in reaching the people. The Saviour mingled with men as one who desired their good. He showed His sympathy for them, ministered to their needs, and won their confidence. Then He bade them, "Follow Me." [Matthew 4:19.][277]

If the followers of Christ were awake to duty, there would be thousands where there is one today proclaiming the Gospel in heathen lands. And all who could not personally engage in the work, would yet sustain it with their means, their sympathy, and their prayers. And there would be far more earnest labor for souls in Christian countries.[278]

There are many who long for special talent with which to do some wonderful work, while the duties lying close at hand, the performance of which would make the life fragrant, are lost sight of. Let such ones go to work, taking up the work lying directly in their pathway. Success depends not so much on talent as on sanctified energy and willingness. It is not the possession of splendid talents that will enable us to overcome and to serve, but the conscientious performance of daily duties, the lowly spirit, the contented disposition, the unaffected, sincere interest in the welfare of others. If the love of Christ fills the heart, this love will be manifested in the life.[279]

275–*The Youth's Instructor*, June 7, 1894.

276–*Steps to Christ*, p. 77.
277–*The Ministry of Healing*, p. 143.
278–*Steps to Christ*, p. 81.
279–*The Review and Herald*, November 14, 1912.

The greater part of our Saviour's life on Earth was spent in patient toil in the carpenter's shop at Nazareth. Ministering angels attended the Lord of life as He walked side by side with peasants and laborers, unrecognized and unhonored. He was as faithfully fulfilling His mission while working at His humble trade as when He healed the sick or walked upon the storm-tossed waves of Galilee. So in the humblest duties and lowliest positions of life, we may walk and work with Jesus.

The apostle says, "Let every man, wherein he is called, therein abide with God." 1 Corinthians 7:24. The businessman may conduct his business in a way that will glorify his Master because of his fidelity. If he is a true follower of Christ he will carry his religion into everything that is done and reveal to men the spirit of Christ. The mechanic may be a diligent and faithful representative of Him Who toiled in the lowly walks of life among the hills of Galilee. Everyone who names the name of Christ should so work that others, by seeing his good works, may be led to glorify their Creator and Redeemer.[280]

There is need of coming close to the people by personal effort.... The poor are to be relieved, the sick cared for, the sorrowing and the bereaved comforted, the ignorant instructed, the inexperienced counseled. We are to weep with those that weep, and rejoice with those that rejoice. Accompanied by the power of persuasion, the power of prayer, the power of the love of God, this work will not, cannot, be without fruit.[281]

Many have no faith in God and have lost confidence in man. But they appreciate acts of sympathy and helpfulness. As they see one with no inducement of earthly praise or compensation come into their homes, ministering to the sick, feeding the hungry, clothing the naked, comforting the sad, and tenderly pointing all to Him of Whose love and pity the human worker is but the messenger—as they see this, their hearts are touched. Gratitude springs up. Faith is kindled. They see that God cares for them, and they are prepared to listen as His Word is opened.[282]

Prayer for Souls

The disciples prayed with intense earnestness for a fitness to meet men and in their daily intercourse to speak words that would lead sinners to Christ. Putting away all differences, all desire for the supremacy, they came close together in Christian fellowship. They drew nearer and nearer to God, and as they did this they realized what a privilege had been theirs in being permitted to associate so closely with Christ. Sadness filled their hearts as they thought of how many times they had grieved Him by their slowness of comprehension, their failure to understand the lessons that, for their good, He was trying to teach them....

The disciples felt their spiritual need and cried to the Lord for the holy unction that was to fit them for the work of soulsaving. They did not ask for a blessing for themselves merely. They were weighted with the burden of the salvation of souls. They realized that the

---

280–*Steps to Christ*, pp. 81, 82.
281–*The Ministry of Healing*, pp. 143, 144.

282–*The Ministry of Healing*, p. 145.

Gospel was to be carried to the world, and they claimed the power that Christ had promised.[283] In rescuing souls from [Satan's] devices, far more will be accomplished by Christlike, humble prayer than by many words without prayer.[284]

Pray most earnestly for an understanding of the times in which we live, for a fuller conception of His purpose, and for increased efficiency in soulsaving.[285] Do not neglect earnest prayer that you may possess a lowly mind, and that angels of God may go before you to work upon the hearts you are trying to reach, and so soften them by heavenly impressions that your efforts may avail.[286] We are to come to God in faith, and pour out our supplications before him, believing that he will work in our behalf, and in behalf of those we are seeking to save. We are to devote more time to earnest prayer.[287] As we seek to win others to Christ, bearing the burden of souls in our prayers, our own hearts will throb with the quickening influence of God's grace; our own affections will glow with more divine fervor; our whole Christian life will be more of a reality, more earnest, more prayerful.[288]

There are many souls yearning unutterably for light, for assurance and strength beyond what they have been able to grasp. They need to be sought out and labored for patiently, perseveringly. Beseech the Lord in fervent prayer for help. Present Jesus because you know Him as your personal Saviour. Let His melting love, His rich grace, flow forth from human lips. You need not present doctrinal points unless questioned. But take the Word, and with tender, yearning love for souls, show them the precious righteousness of Christ, to Whom you and they must come to be saved.[289]

You are to be the agent through whom God will speak to the soul. Precious things will be brought to your remembrance, and with a heart overflowing with the love of Jesus, you will speak words of vital interest and import. Your simplicity and sincerity will be the highest eloquence, and your words will be registered in the books of Heaven as fit words, which are like apples of gold in pictures of silver. God will make them a healing flood of heavenly influence, awakening conviction and desire, and Jesus will add His intercession to your prayers, and claim for the sinner the gift of the Holy Spirit, and pour it upon his soul.[290]

The Law of Love

When the love of Christ is enshrined in the heart, like sweet fragrance it cannot be hidden. Its holy influence will be felt by all with whom we come in contact.[291] The sweet savor of Christ will surround us, and our influence will elevate and bless.[292] The Spirit of Christ in the heart is like a spring in the desert, flowing to refresh all and making those who are ready to perish, eager to drink of the water of life.[293] The love of

---

283–*The Acts of the Apostles*, p. 37.
284–*Colporteur Ministry*, p. 81.
285–*The Review and Herald*, May 29, 1913.
286–*Testimonies for the Church*, vol. 2, p. 53.
287–*The Review and Herald*, April 29, 1909.
288–*Christ's Object Lessons*, 354.
289–*Evangelism*, p. 442.
290–*Sons and Daughters of God*, p. 274.
291–*Steps to Christ*, p. 77.
292–*Steps to Christ*, p. 82.
293–*Steps to Christ*, p. 77.

Christ, revealed to us, makes us debtors to all who know Him not. God has given us light, not for ourselves alone, but to shed upon them.²⁹⁴

The two great principles of the law of God are supreme love to God and unselfish love to our neighbor. The first four commandments, and the last six, hang upon, or grow out of, these two principles. Christ explained to the lawyer who was his neighbor, in the illustration of the man who was traveling from Jerusalem to Jericho and fell among thieves who robbed him, and beat him, and left him half dead. The priest and the Levite saw this man suffering, but their hearts did not respond to his wants. They avoided him by passing by on the other side. The Samaritan came that way, and when he saw the stranger's need of help, he did not question whether he was of their country, or of their creed, or a relative; but he went to work to help the sufferer because there was work which needed to be done. He relieved him as best he could, put him upon his own beast and carried him to an inn, and made provision for his wants at the expense of his own purse. The Samaritan, said Christ, was neighbor to him who fell among thieves. The Levite and the priest represent a class who manifest an indifference to the very ones who need their sympathy and help. The Samaritan represents a class who are true helpers with Christ, and are imitating His example in doing good. This class Christ represents as commandment keepers, who shall have eternal life.²⁹⁵

Laziness

Many have excused themselves from rendering their gifts to the service of Christ because others were possessed of superior endowments and advantages. The opinion has prevailed that only those who are especially talented are required to consecrate their abilities to the service of God. It has come to be understood by many that talents are given to only a certain favored class to the exclusion of others who of course are not called upon to share in the toils or the rewards. But it is not so represented in the parable [of the talents]. When the master of the house called his servants, he gave to every man his work.²⁹⁶ Everyone, to the extent of his talent and opportunity, is to fulfill the Saviour's commission.²⁹⁷ The Lord calls all who believe in Him to be workers together with Him.²⁹⁸

Intellectual laziness and spiritual lethargy must be overcome, and as Christ's soldiers we must be faithful to duty, ready for every good work.²⁹⁹ You are not to wait for great occasions or to expect extraordinary abilities before you go to work for God. You need not have a thought of what the world will think of you.³⁰⁰ The Christian must lay aside all selfishness, living and working for the good of others. The only way to grow in grace is to do the work that Christ has enjoined upon us, helping and blessing those who need the help we can give. Strength comes by exercise; action is

---

294–*Steps to Christ*, p. 81.
295–*The Signs of the Times*, August 3, 1876.

296–*Steps to Christ*, p. 82.
297–*Steps to Christ*, p. 81.
298–*Christ Triumphant*, p. 360.
299–*The Review and Herald*, January 2, 1879.
300–*Steps to Christ*, p. 83.

the very condition of life. Those who endeavor to maintain Christian life by passively accepting the blessings that come through the means of grace, and doing nothing for Christ, are trying to live by eating without working. And in the spiritual as in the natural world, this always results in degeneration and decay. A man who would refuse to exercise his limbs would soon lose the power to use them. The Christian who will not exercise his God-given powers, not only fails of growing up into Christ, but he loses the strength that he already had.[301]

The Saviour's life on Earth was not a life of ease and devotion to Himself, but He toiled with persistent, earnest, untiring effort for the salvation of lost mankind. From the manger to Calvary He followed the path of self-denial and sought not to be released from arduous tasks, painful travels and exhausting care and labor. He said, "The Son of Man came not to be ministered unto, but to minister, and to give His life a ransom for many." Matthew 20:28. This was the one great object of His life. Everything else was secondary and subservient. It was His meat and drink to do the will of God and to finish His work. Self and self-interest had no part in His labor.[302]

Blessing

The humblest and poorest of the disciples of Jesus can be a blessing to others. They may not realize that they are doing any special good, but by their unconscious influence they may start waves of blessing that will widen and deepen, and the blessed results they may never know until the day of final reward. They do not feel or know that they are doing anything great. They are not required to weary themselves with anxiety about success. They have only to go forward quietly, doing faithfully the work that God's providence assigns, and their life will not be in vain. Their own souls will be growing more and more into the likeness of Christ; they are workers together with God in this life and are thus fitting for the higher work and the unshadowed joy of the life to come.[303]

The beams of Heaven's attractive loveliness are to shine forth from us, showing the only good and right way, and ever showing the superiority of God's law above every human enactment. Bible religion is not to be hidden away in the dark. It delights to be examined.[304] The effort to bless others will react in blessings upon ourselves. This was the purpose of God in giving us a part to act in the plan of redemption. He has granted men the privilege of becoming partakers of the divine nature and, in their turn, of diffusing blessings to their fellow men. This is the highest honor, the greatest joy, that it is possible for God to bestow upon men. Those who thus become participants in labors of love are brought nearest to their Creator.[305]

Many who see the work for this time, and realize its importance, are pressed under the weight of responsibility as a cart beneath sheaves, while hundreds are dying a spiritual death of inaction because they will not work at all. These

---

301–*The Signs of the Times*, March 19, 1902.
302–*Steps to Christ*, p. 78.
303–*Steps to Christ*, p. 83.
304–*The Youth's Instructor*, March 4, 1897.
305–*Steps to Christ*, p. 79.

might come into working order if they would gather divine strength, and yield not to passing influences. They have the opportunity to cultivate traits of character which would be the opposite of selfishness, which would refine, enrich, and ennoble their lives. These may grow in spirituality if they will accept any burdens of the work where they can best serve the cause of God. Christians, in the fullest acceptation of the term, grow in grace and in the knowledge of Jesus Christ. They love God more and more, and are more and more desirous of acting a part in the great plan of salvation. Intellectual laziness and spiritual lethargy must be overcome, and as Christ's soldiers we must be faithful to duty, ready for every good work.[306]

The Fellowship of Christ's Sufferings

All who would work for the Master must submit to the yoke of Christ. This submission involves self-sacrifice and entire consecration of body, soul, and spirit. As they learn of Christ, His meekness and lowliness, they will find that His yoke is easy and His burden is light.[307] When self dies, there will be awakened an intense desire for the salvation of others,—a desire which will lead to persevering efforts to do good. There will be a sowing beside all waters; and earnest supplication, importunate prayers, will enter Heaven in behalf of perishing souls.[308]

We are brought into sympathy with Christ through the fellowship of His sufferings. Every act of self-sacrifice for the good of others strengthens the spirit of beneficence in the giver's heart, allying him more closely to the Redeemer of the world, Who "was rich, yet for your sakes ... became poor, that ye through His poverty might be rich." 2 Corinthians 8:9. And it is only as we thus fulfill the divine purpose in our creation that life can be a blessing to us.[309]

If the Christian thrives and progresses at all, he must do so amid strangers to God, amid scoffing, subject to ridicule. He must stand upright, like the palm tree in the desert. The sky may be as brass, the desert sand may beat about the palm tree's roots, and pile itself in heaps about its trunk. Yet the tree lives as an evergreen, fresh and vigorous amid the burning desert sands. Remove the sand till you reach the rootlets of the palm tree, and you discover the secret of its life; it strikes down deep beneath the surface, to the secret waters hidden in the earth. Christians indeed may be fitly represented by the palm tree. They are like Enoch; although surrounded with corrupting influences their faith takes hold of the Unseen. They walk with God, deriving strength and grace from Him to withstand the moral pollution surrounding them. Like Daniel in the courts of Babylon, they stand pure and uncontaminated; their life is hid with Christ in God. They are virtuous in spirit amid depravity; they are true and loyal, fervent and zealous, while surrounded by infidels, hypocritical professors, godless and worldly men. Their faith and life are hid with Christ in God. Jesus is in them a well of water springing up into everlasting

---

306–*The Review and Herald*, January 2, 1879.
307–*Christ Triumphant*, p. 360.
308–*Gospel Workers*, 470.

309–*Steps to Christ*, pp. 79, 80.

life. Faith, like the rootlets of the palm tree, penetrates beneath the things which are seen, drawing spiritual nourishment from the Fountain of life.[310]

Those who are the partakers of the grace of Christ will be ready to make any sacrifice, that others for whom He died may share the heavenly gift. They will do all they can to make the world better for their stay in it. This spirit is the sure outgrowth of a soul truly converted. No sooner does one come to Christ than there is born in his heart a desire to make known to others what a precious Friend he has found in Jesus; the saving and sanctifying truth cannot be shut up in his heart. If we are clothed with the righteousness of Christ and are filled with the joy of His indwelling Spirit, we shall not be able to hold our peace. If we have tasted and seen that the Lord is good we shall have something to tell. Like Philip when he found the Saviour, we shall invite others into His presence. We shall seek to present to them the attractions of Christ and the unseen realities of the world to come. There will be an intensity of desire to follow in the path that Jesus trod. There will be an earnest longing that those around us may "behold the Lamb of God, Which taketh away the sin of the world." John 1:29.[311]

Growing in Christ

God might have committed the message of the Gospel, and all the work of loving ministry, to the heavenly angels. He might have employed other means for accomplishing His purpose. But in His infinite love He chose to make us coworkers with Himself, with Christ and the angels, that we might share the blessing, the joy, the spiritual uplifting, which results from this unselfish ministry.[312]

Every provision has been made that we may attain a height of stature in Christ Jesus that will meet the divine standard. God is not pleased with His representatives if they are content to be dwarfs when they might grow up to the full stature of men and women in Christ. He wants you to have height and breadth in Christian experience. He wants you to have great thoughts, noble aspirations, clear perceptions of truth, and lofty purposes of action. Every passing year should increase the soul's yearning for purity and perfection of Christian character.... We are to work for the great Taskmaster's eye, whether our painstaking efforts are seen and appreciated by men or not. No man, woman, nor child can acceptably serve God with neglectful, haphazard, sham work, whether it be secular or religious service. The true Christian will have an eye single to the glory of God in all things, encouraging His purposes and strengthening His principles with this thought, "I do this for Christ."[313]

If you will go to work as Christ designs that His disciples shall, and win souls for Him, you will feel the need of a deeper experience and a greater knowledge in divine things, and will hunger and thirst after righteousness. You will plead with God, and your faith will be strengthened, and your soul will drink deeper drafts at the well of salvation. Encountering opposition and

---

310–*The Review and Herald*, January 2, 1879.
311–*Steps to Christ*, pp. 78, 79.
312–*Steps to Christ*, p. 79.
313–*The Review and Herald*, December 16, 1884.

trials will drive you to the Bible and prayer. You will grow in grace and the knowledge of Christ, and will develop a rich experience.[314]

---

[314]–*Steps to Christ*, p. 80.

Chapter 13

Pray for One Another

Prayer Is the Answer

Keep your wants, your joys, your sorrows, your cares, and your fears before God.... There is no chapter in our experience too dark for Him to read; there is no perplexity too difficult for Him to unravel. No calamity can befall the least of His children, no anxiety harass the soul, no joy cheer, no sincere prayer escape the lips, of which our Heavenly Father is unobservant, or in which He takes no immediate interest.[315]

Christ always knows what is cherished in the heart. We must come in faith that the Lord will hear and answer our prayers; for "whatsoever is not of faith is sin." [Romans 14:23.] Genuine faith is the faith that works by love, and purifies the soul.[316] The life of the soul depends upon habitual communion with God. Its wants are made known, and the heart is open to receive fresh blessings. Gratitude flows from unfeigned lips; and the refreshing that is received from Jesus is manifested in words, in deeds of active benevolence, and in public devotion. There is love to Jesus in the heart; and where love exists, it will not be repressed, but will express itself. Secret prayer sustains this inner life. The heart that loves God will desire to commune with Him, and will lean on Him in holy confidence.[317]

Prayer is communion with God, the Fountain of wisdom, the Source of strength, and peace, and happiness.[318] Prayer moves the arm of Omnipotence. He Who marshals the stars in order in the heavens, Whose word controls the waves of the great deep—the same Infinite Creator will work in behalf of His people, if they will call upon Him in faith. He will restrain all the forces of darkness, until the warning is given to the world, and all who will heed it are prepared for His coming.[319] Prayer will be no difficult task to the soul that loves God; it will

---

315–*Steps to Christ*, p. 100.
316–*The Youth's Instructor*, September 13, 1894.
317–*The Review and Herald*, April 22, 1884.
318–*Child Guidance*, p. 518.
319–*The Review and Herald*, December 14, 1905.

be a pleasure, a source of strength.[320] The idea that prayer is not essential is one of Satan's most successful devices to ruin souls.[321]

Those who do not learn every day in the school of Christ, who do not spend much time in earnest prayer, are not fit to handle the work of God in any of its branches; for if they do, human depravity will surely overcome them and they will lift up their souls unto vanity. Those who become coworkers with Jesus Christ, and who have spirituality to discern spiritual things, will feel their need of virtue and of wisdom from Heaven in handling His work.[322] Every worker who follows the example of Christ will be prepared to receive and use the power that God has promised to His church for the ripening of Earth's harvest. Morning by morning, those who kneel before the Lord and renew their vows of consecration to Him, He will grant them the presence of His Spirit, with its reviving, sanctifying power. As they go forth to the day's duties, they have the assurance that the unseen agency of the Holy Spirit enables them to be "laborers together with God." [1 Corinthians 3:9.]

Into God's Presence

The tenderness of Christ must pervade the heart of the worker. If you have a love for souls you will reveal a tender solicitude for them. You will offer humble, earnest, heartfelt prayers for those whom you visit. The fragrance of Christ's love will be revealed in your work. He Who gave His Own life for the life of the world will cooperate with the unselfish worker to make an impression upon human hearts.[323] Let us ... pray for one another, bringing one another right into the presence of God by living faith.[324]

Begin to pray for souls; come near to Christ, close to His bleeding side. Let a meek and quiet spirit adorn your lives, and let your earnest, broken, humble petitions ascend to Him for wisdom that you may have success in saving not only your own soul, but the souls of others.[325] As workers for God we want more of Jesus and less of self. We should have more of a burden for souls, and should pray daily that strength and wisdom may be given us.... Let the heart be softened, and the petitions short and simple, but earnest.[326]

Too often we forget that our fellow laborers are in need of strength and cheer. In times of special perplexity and burden, take care to assure them of your interest and sympathy. While you try to help them by your prayers, let them know that you do it. Send along the line God's message to His workers: "Be strong and of a good courage." Joshua 1:6.[327]

There are those all around you who have woes, who need words of sympathy, love, and tenderness, and our humble, pitying prayers.[328] The Lord turned the captivity of Job when he prayed, not only for himself, but for those who were opposing him. When he felt earnestly

---

320–*The Review and Herald*, May 13, 1884.
321–*Child Guidance*, p. 518.
322–*Testimonies to Ministers and Gospel Workers*, p. 169.
323–*Testimonies for the Church*, vol. 6, pp. 75, 76.
324–*The Review and Herald*, August 28, 1888.
325–*Testimonies for the Church*, vol. 1, p. 513.
326–*Counsels on Sabbath School Work*, p. 125.
327–*Testimonies for the Church*, vol. 7, p. 185.
328–*Testimonies for the Church*, vol. 3, p. 530.

desirous that the souls that had trespassed against him might be helped, he himself received help. Let us pray, not only for ourselves, but for those who have hurt us, and are continuing to hurt us. Pray, pray, especially in your mind. Give not the Lord rest; for His ears are open to hear sincere, importunate prayers, when the soul is humbled before Him.[329]

The Family of Man

We are to ask that we may give. The principle of Christ's life must be the principle of our lives. "For their sakes," He said, speaking of His disciples, "I sanctify Myself, that they also might be sanctified." John 17:19. The same devotion, the same self-sacrifice, the same subjection to the claims of the Word of God, that were manifest in Christ, must be seen in His servants. Our mission to the world is not to serve or please ourselves; we are to glorify God by cooperating with Him to save sinners. We are to ask blessings from God that we may communicate to others. The capacity for receiving is preserved only by imparting. We cannot continue to receive heavenly treasure without communicating to those around us.[330] When we pray, "Give us this day our daily bread [Matthew 6:11]," we ask for others as well as ourselves. And we acknowledge that what God gives us is not for ourselves alone. God gives to us in trust, that we may feed the hungry.[331]

We are all a part of the great web of humanity, all members of one family. In our petitions we are to include our neighbors as well as ourselves. No one prays aright who seeks a blessing for himself alone.[332] There are many from whom hope has departed. Bring back the sunshine to them. Many have lost their courage. Speak to them words of cheer. Pray for them.[333] There are those who need the Bread of Life. Read to them from the Word of God. There is a soul sickness no balm can reach, no medicine heal. Pray for these, and bring them to Jesus Christ. And in all your work Christ will be present to make impressions upon human hearts.[334]

Earnest appeals are to be made. Fervent prayers are to be offered. Our tame, spiritless petitions are to be changed into petitions of intense earnestness.[335] Learning, talent, eloquence, every natural or acquired endowment, may be possessed; but without the presence of the Spirit of God, no heart will be touched, no sinner won to Christ. On the other hand, if they are connected with Christ, if the gifts of the Spirit are theirs, the poorest and most ignorant of His disciples will have power that will tell upon hearts. God makes them channels for the outflowing of the highest influence in the universe.[336] Let there be far more wrestling with God for the salvation of souls. Work disinterestedly, determinedly, with a spirit never to let go. Compel souls to come in to the marriage supper of the

---

329–*Letter 88*, 1906.
330–*Christ's Object Lessons*, pp. 142, 143.
331–*Thoughts From the Mount of Blessing*, pp. 111, 112.
332–*Sons and Daughters of God*, p. 267.
333–*Prophets and Kings*, p. 719.
334–*Welfare Ministry*, p. 71.
335–*Testimonies for the Church*, vol. 7, p. 12.
336–*The Review and Herald*, April 30, 1908.

The Prayer of Daniel

An earnest prayer offered from a contrite heart by one who desires to do the Master's will is of more value in God's sight than is eloquence of speech.... The King of kings bends low to listen to the prayer coming from a humble, contrite heart. God hears every prayer that is offered with the incense of faith. The weakest child of God may exert an influence in harmony with the councils of Heaven.[338]

If we would offer acceptable prayer, there is a work to be done in confessing our sins to one another.... Daniel's example of prayer and confession is given for our instruction and encouragement.[339]

"I set my face unto the Lord God, to seek by prayer and supplications, with fasting, and sackcloth, and ashes: And I prayed unto the Lord my God, and made my confession, and said, O Lord, the great and dreadful God, keeping the covenant and mercy to them that love Him, and to them that keep His commandments; we have sinned, and have committed iniquity, and have done wickedly, and have rebelled, even by departing from thy precepts and from thy judgments: Neither have we hearkened unto thy servants the prophets, which spake in thy name to our kings, our princes, and our fathers, and to all the people of the land.... We have sinned against Thee.... We have rebelled against Him; neither have we obeyed the voice of the Lord our God, to walk in His laws, which He set before us by His servants the prophets. Yea, all Israel have transgressed Thy law, even by departing, that they might not obey Thy voice ... because we have sinned against Him.... Yet made we not our prayer before the Lord our God, that we might turn from our iniquities, and understand Thy truth.... For we obeyed not His voice.... We have sinned, we have done wickedly.

"Now therefore, O our God, hear the prayer of Thy servant, and his supplications, and cause Thy face to shine upon Thy sanctuary that is desolate, for the Lord's sake.... We do not present our supplications before Thee for our righteousness, but for Thy great mercies. O Lord, hear; O Lord, forgive; O Lord, hearken and do; defer not, for Thine Own sake, O my God: for Thy city and Thy people are called by Thy name."[340] Prayer will draw down from Heaven great blessings when those who claim to believe the truth shall come down from their stilts of self-exaltation and afflict their souls, even as Daniel afflicted his soul.[341]

The prophet Daniel was drawing very near to God when he was seeking Him with confession and humiliation of soul. He did not try to excuse himself or his people, but acknowledged the full extent of their transgression. In their behalf he confessed sins of which he himself was not guilty, and besought the mercy of God, that he might bring his brethren to see their sins, and with him

---

337–*Testimonies for the Church*, vol. 6, p. 66.
338–*That I May Know Him*, p. 270.
339–*The Review and Herald*, February 9, 1897.
340–Daniel 9:3–19.
341–*Manuscript Releases*, vol. 11, pp. 178, 179.

to humble their hearts before the Lord.[342] Daniel makes no plea on the ground of his own goodness; but he says: "O my God, incline Thine ear, and hear; open Thine eyes, and behold our desolations, and the city which is called by Thy name: for we do not present our supplications before Thee for our righteousness, but for Thy great mercies." His intensity of desire makes him earnest and fervent. He continues: "O Lord, hear; O Lord, forgive; O Lord, hearken and do; defer not, for Thine Own sake, O my God; for Thy city and Thy people are called by Thy name." [Daniel 9:18.][343]

Prayer for the Wayward

Those who walk in the light will see signs of the approaching peril; but they are not to sit in quiet, unconcerned expectancy of the ruin, comforting themselves with the belief that God will shelter His people in the day of visitation. Far from it. They should realize that it is their duty to labor diligently to save others, looking with strong faith to God for help. "The effectual, fervent prayer of a righteous man availeth much." James 5:16.

The leaven of godliness has not entirely lost its power. At the time when the danger and depression of the church are greatest, the little company who are standing in the light will be sighing and crying for the abominations that are done in the land. But more especially will their prayers arise in behalf of the church, because its members are doing after the manner of the world.[344]

"We pray always for you, that our God would count you worthy of this calling, and fulfill all the good pleasure of His goodness, and the work of faith with power."[345] Therefore I exhort first of all that supplications, prayers, intercessions, and giving of thanks be made for all men, for kings and all who are in authority, that we may lead a quiet and peaceable life in all godliness and reverence.[346]

If those who sound the solemn notes of warning for this time could realize their accountability to God, they would see the necessity for fervent prayer. When the cities were hushed in midnight slumber, when every man had gone to his own house, Christ, our Example, would repair to the Mount of Olives, and there, amid the overshadowing trees, would spend the entire night in prayer. He Who was Himself without the taint of sin,—a treasure house of blessing; whose voice was heard in the fourth watch of the night by the terrified disciples upon the stormy sea, in heavenly benediction; and Whose word could summon the dead from their graves,—He it was Who made supplication with strong crying and tears. He prayed not for Himself, but for those whom He came to save. As He became a suppliant, seeking at the hand of His Father fresh supplies of strength, and coming forth refreshed and invigorated as man's substitute, He identified Himself with suffering humanity, and gave them an example of the necessity of prayer.

342–*The Review and Herald*, December 16, 1890.
343–*The Review and Herald*, February 9, 1897.
344–*Christian Experience and Teachings of Ellen G. White*, pp. 186, 187.
345–2 Thessalonians 1:11.
346–1 Timothy 2:1, 2.

His nature was without the taint of sin. As the Son of Man, He prayed to the Father, showing that human nature requires all the divine support which man can obtain that he may be braced for duty and prepared for trial. As the Prince of Life, He had power with God, and prevailed for His people. This Saviour, Who prayed for those that felt no need of prayer, and wept for those that felt no need of tears, is now before the throne, to receive and present to His Father the petitions of those for whom He prayed on Earth. The example of Christ is for us to follow. Prayer is a necessity in our labor for the salvation of souls. God alone can give the increase of the seed we sow."[347]

---

[347]–*Gospel Workers*, pp. 28, 29.

Chapter 14

In His Name

Building

"There is none other name under heaven given among men, whereby we must be saved." [Acts 4:12.] Christ the Word, the revelation of God,—the manifestation of His character, His law, His love, His life,—is the only foundation upon which we can build a character that will endure.

We build on Christ by obeying His word. It is not he who merely enjoys righteousness, that is righteous, but he who does righteousness. Holiness is not rapture; it is the result of surrendering all to God; it is doing the will of our Heavenly Father. Religion consists in doing the words of Christ; not doing to earn God's favor, but because, all undeserving, we have received the gift of His love. Christ places the salvation of man, not upon profession merely, but upon faith that is made manifest in works of righteousness. "As many as are led by the Spirit of God, they are the sons of God." [Romans 8:14.] Not those whose hearts are touched by the Spirit, not those who now and then yield to Its power, but they that are led by the Spirit, are the sons of God. To live by the word of God means the surrender to Him of the whole life.

There will be felt a continual sense of need and dependence, a drawing out of the heart after God.[348] It was in the mount with God that Moses beheld the pattern of that wonderful building that was to be the abiding place of God's glory. It is in the mount with God,—in the secret place of communion,—that we are to contemplate His glorious ideal for humanity. Thus we shall be able so to fashion our character building that to us may be fulfilled his promise. "I will dwell in them, and walk in them; and I will be their God, and they shall be My people." [2 Corinthians 6:16.][349]

348–*The Review and Herald*, December 31, 1908.
349–*The Review and Herald*, December 31, 1908.

Take the Name

Those who take the name of Christian should come to God in earnestness and humility, pleading for help. The Saviour has told us to pray without ceasing. The Christian cannot always be in the position of prayer, but his thoughts and desires can always be upward. Our self-confidence would vanish, did we talk less and pray more.

We give evidence of the sincerity of our prayers by the earnestness of our endeavors to answer them, to overcome the sins which strive for a place in the life. Our prayers will be ineffectual unless we continually strive to correct that which is wrong and unlovely in our lives. If we ask God to work for us, and then make no effort to conquer self, our prayers will rise no higher than our heads. God helps those who cooperate with Him. We can obtain forgiveness only through the blood of Christ. His atoning sacrifice is all-powerful. But in the struggle for immortality we have a part to act. Christ will help those who pray and then watch unto prayer. He calls upon us to use every power He has given us in the warfare against sin. We can never be saved in inactivity and idleness. We might as well look for a harvest from seed which we have not sown, and for knowledge where we have not studied, as to expect salvation without making an effort. It is our part to wrestle against the evil tendencies of the natural heart.[350]

Heaven's Treasury

God designs us to find a place in the heavenly temple.[351] Our Heavenly Father waits to bestow upon us the fullness of His blessing.[352] God has opened to us all the treasures of Heaven through the precious gift of His Son, Who is fully able to uplift, ennoble, and fit us, through His perfection of character, for usefulness in this life and for a holy Heaven.[353] God's appointments and grants in our behalf are without limit.

The throne of grace is itself the highest attraction because [it is] occupied by One Who permits us to call Him Father. But God did not deem the principle of salvation complete while invested only with His Own love. By His appointment He has placed at His altar an Advocate clothed with our nature. As our Intercessor, His office work is to introduce us to God as His sons and daughters. Christ intercedes in behalf of those who have received Him. To them He gives power, by virtue of His Own merits, to become members of the royal family, children of the heavenly King. And the Father demonstrates His infinite love for Christ, Who paid our ransom with His blood, by receiving and welcoming Christ's friends as His friends. He is satisfied with the atonement made. He is glorified by the incarnation, the life, death, and mediation of His Son.

No sooner does the child of God approach the mercy seat than he becomes the client of the great Advocate. At his first utterance of penitence and appeal

---

350–*The Youth's Instructor*, March 5, 1903.

351–*Testimonies for the Church*, vol. 6, p. 363.
352–*Steps to Christ*, p. 94.
353–*Testimonies for the Church*, vol. 5, p. 579.

for pardon Christ espouses his case and makes it His Own, presenting the supplication before the Father as His Own request.

As Christ intercedes in our behalf, the Father lays open all the treasures of His grace for our appropriation, to be enjoyed and to be communicated to others.[354] The whole treasury of Heaven is open to those He seeks to save. Having collected the riches of the universe, and laid open the resources of infinite power, He gives them all into the hands of Christ, and says, All these are for man. Use these gifts to convince him that there is no love greater than Mine in Earth or Heaven. His greatest happiness will be found in loving Me.[355]

We are to present our requests to God in faith, asking for the very things which we know that we need. When we have a sense of what God is, we shall realize our own unworthiness; but we shall also have confidence toward God, knowing what is His character of mercy and love. We shall come into His presence through the merits of Christ, and through Him have boldness and confidence.[356] Faith is the key that opens the divine treasury, is the hand by which we appropriate to our use the richest gifts of God. The prayer of the contrite heart unlocks the treasure house of supplies, and lays hold of Omnipotent Power. This kind of prayer enables the supplicant to understand what it means to lay hold of the strength of God, and to make peace with Him. . . .

It is our privilege and duty to bring the efficacy of the name of Christ into our petitions, and use the very arguments that Christ has used in our behalf. Our prayers will then be in complete harmony with the will of God. Then it is that Christ clothes the contrite suppliant with His Own priestly vestments, and the human petitioner approaches the altar holding the holy censer, from which ascends the incense of the fragrance of the merit of Christ's righteousness.

Our Redeemer encourages us to present continual supplications. He makes to us most decided promises that we shall not plead in vain. He says: "Ask, and it shall be given you; seek, and ye shall find; knock, and it shall be opened unto you. For everyone that asketh receiveth; and he that seeketh findeth; and to him that knocketh it shall be opened." [Matthew 7:7, 8.][357]

The Gift of His Life

God has made provision that we may become like unto Him, and He will accomplish this for all who do not interpose a perverse will and thus frustrate His grace.[358] [Jesus] came to unite man with God, to impart divine strength to the repenting soul, and from the manger to Calvary to pass over the path which man would travel, at every step giving man a perfect example of what he should do, presenting in His character what humanity might become when united with Divinity.[359] Christ in His humanity wrought out a perfect char-

---

354–*Testimonies for the Church*, vol. 6, p. 364.
355–*The Desire of Ages*, p. 57.
356–*The Review and Herald*, May 28, 1895.

357–*The Signs of the Times*, December 23, 1889.
358–*Thoughts From the Mount of Blessing*, p. 76.
359–*The Bible Echo*, November 1, 1892.

acter, and this character He offers to impart to us.[360]

His Name

The disciples were unacquainted with the Saviour's unlimited resources and power. He said to them, "Hitherto have ye asked nothing in My name." John 16:24. He explained that the secret of their success would be in asking for strength and grace in His name. He would be present before the Father to make requests for them. The prayer of the humble suppliant He presents as His Own desire in that soul's behalf. Every sincere prayer is heard in Heaven. It may not be fluently expressed; but if the heart is in it, it will ascend to the sanctuary where Jesus ministers, and He will present it to the Father without one awkward, stammering word, beautiful and fragrant with the incense of His Own perfection.[361]

Jesus has given us His name, above every name. "Whatsoever ye shall ask in My name," says Christ, "that will I do, that the Father may be glorified in the Son. If ye shall ask anything in My name, I will do it. If ye love Me, keep My commandments." "I have chosen you, and ordained you, that ye should go and bring forth fruit, and that your fruit should remain; that whatsoever ye shall ask of the Father in My name, He may give it you." "Hitherto have ye asked nothing in My name; ask, and ye shall receive, that your joy may be full." "At that day ye shall ask in My name; and I say not unto you that I will pray the Father for you; for the Father Himself loveth you, because ye have loved Me, and have believed that I came out from God." [John 14:13–15; 15:16; 16:24, 26, 27.]

We have a string of precious pearls in the promises, if we will but comply with the conditions. But to pray in the name of Jesus is something more than a mere mention of that name at the beginning and ending of a prayer. It is to pray in the mind and Spirit of Jesus, while we work His works, believe His promises, and rely on His matchless grace.[362]

To pray in Christ's name means much. It means that we are to accept His character, manifest His Spirit, and work His works. The Saviour's promise is given on condition. "If ye love Me," He says, "keep My commandments." [John 14:15.] He saves men, not in sin, but from sin; and those who love Him will show their love by obedience.[363]

God did not design that His wonderful plan to redeem men should achieve only insignificant results. All who will go to work, trusting not in what they themselves can do, but in what God can do for and through them, will certainly realize the fulfillment of His promise. "Greater works than these shall ye do," He declares; "because I go unto My Father." [John 14:12b.][364]

The Gift of His Life

"Verily, verily, I say unto you," Christ continued, "He that believeth on Me, the works that I do shall he do also." [John 14:12a.]

360–*The Signs of the Times*, November 22, 1905.
361–*The Review and Herald*, November 23, 1905.
362–*The Signs of the Times*, August 21, 1884.
363–*The Review and Herald*, November 23, 1905.
364–*The Desire of Ages*, p. 664.

The Saviour was deeply anxious for His disciples to understand for what purpose His divinity was united to humanity. He came to the world to display the glory of God, that man might be uplifted by its restoring power. God was manifested in Him that He might be manifested in them. Jesus revealed no qualities, and exercised no powers, that men may not have through faith in Him. His perfect humanity is that which all His followers may possess, if they will be in subjection to God as He was.[365]

Nothing short of unreserved consecration to God will place us in such a relation to Him that we will rightly perform every daily duty, and cultivate a piety so thorough and practical as to make itself felt by all in the circle of our influence…. We must study the example Christ has left us, as revealed in His character; and then, all unconsciously to ourselves, we shall do the works He did.[366]

The Gift of His Presence

Unceasing prayer is the unbroken union of the soul with God, so that life from God flows into our life; and from our life, purity and holiness flow back to God.[367] If we consent, He will so identify Himself with our thoughts and aims, so blend our hearts and minds into conformity to His will, that when obeying Him we shall be but carrying out our own impulses. The will, refined and sanctified, will find its highest delight in doing His service. When we know God as it is our privilege to know Him, our life will be a life of continual obedience. Through an appreciation of the character of Christ, through communion with God, sin will become hateful to us.[368]

365–*The Desire of Ages*, p. 664.
366–*The Review and Herald*, November 16, 1886.
367–*Steps to Christ*, p. 97.
368–*The Review and Herald*, November 23, 1905.

Chapter 15

Judgment

Friend and Saviour

Jesus did not come to the world as a judge, but as the Friend and Saviour of sinners. "God so loved the world, that he gave His Only-Begotten Son, that whosoever believeth in Him should not perish, but have everlasting life. For God sent not His Son into the world to condemn the world; but that the world through Him might be saved."[369] [John 3:16, 17.] God has not given men the power to read hearts. He has not placed them in the judgment seat, to pass sentence upon their fellow men. God has committed all judgment to His Son. Why, then, are human beings not more careful in regard to passing judgment upon one another? Let us seek to realize our own ignorance. When we have a full realization of this, we shall not speak evil of our brethren.[370]

Criticism & Condemnation

When Christ came into the world, it was filled with criticism and condemnation of others, and Jesus revealed the sure result of such a course. The same results are manifest today. Those who have the greatest need to examine themselves whether they be in the faith, are most forward to pronounce sentence of evil against their brethren. Those who are accusers of the brethren are recipients of God's mercy and compassion, are every moment dependent upon His care and benevolence, and yet they are unmerciful to others, making it manifest that they have not allowed the truth to purify, refine, and sanctify them. Our characters are not to be weighed by smooth words and fair speeches manufactured for set times and occasions; but by the spirit and trend of the whole life. The unkind man, the critic, the one who is full of self-conceit, deceives his own soul, though claiming to be a clear discerner of the defects of others. He who has a disposition to

---

369–*The Signs of the Times*, March 21, 1892.
370–*The Review and Herald*, October 29, 1901.

find fault, to be suspicious, to surmise, think and speak evil, has so cultivated this attribute of the evil one that the good qualities of his brethren and sisters in the church do not arrest his attention. If he thinks he has discovered a flaw in the character, a mistake in the life, he is very officious to aim at the mote, when the very trait of character which he has overlooked in himself, which is developed in doing this un-Christlike work, is, in comparison to what he criticizes, when weighed in the golden balances of Heaven as a beam in proportion to a mote.[371]

How can the professed followers of Christ manifest so little of the tender mercy and compassion of their Lord? If there is in their number one even of perverse disposition, one who makes them trouble, how can they feel at liberty to cut him off from the church so readily, and treat him as an alien and an outcast? Let us be careful how we hurt and bruise the souls of men and women for whom Christ died.[372] If Christ is in you "the Hope of glory" [Colossians 1:28], you will have no disposition to watch others, to expose their errors. Instead of seeking to accuse and condemn, it will be your object to help, to bless, and to save. In dealing with those who are in error, you will heed the injunction, Consider "thyself, lest thou also be tempted." Galatians 6:1. You will call to mind the many times you have erred and how hard it was to find the right way when you had once left it. You will not push your brother into greater darkness, but with a heart full of pity will tell him of his danger.[373] If men could see themselves as God sees them, they would have such a sense of their own weakness and defects, and would see such a work to be done for themselves, they would have such a sense of their own need of the long-suffering mercy of God, and the forbearance of their fellow men, that they would have no disposition to judge and condemn others.[374]

Mercy and Love

To the repenting sinner, God is ever ready to show His mercy and truth; He is ready to bestow upon him forgiveness and love; and He requires that those who have been blessed by His compassion, shall reveal the same mercy and love toward their fellow men; for this is doing the works of Christ, this is keeping the commandments of God. Those who show true gratitude glorify God by loving Him supremely and their neighbors as themselves. They manifest the fact that they have received not the spirit which is of the world, but the Spirit Which is of God.[375]

The Lord pardons all who repent of their sins. It is from those who do not repent, those who bolster themselves up in self-confidence, that He turns away. Never will He refuse to listen to the voice of tears and repentance. Never will He turn His face away from the humble soul who comes to Him in repentance and sorrow. . . .

371–*The Review and Herald*, August 16, 1892.
372–*The Signs of the Times*, March 21, 1892.
373–*Thoughts From the Mount of Blessing*, p. 128.
374–*The Signs of the Times*, March 14, 1892.
375–*The Signs of the Times*, July 11, 1892.

The church member who believes the Word of God will never look indifferently upon a soul that humbles himself and confesses his sin. Let the repenting one be taken back with rejoicing. Christ came to the world to forgive everyone who says, "I repent. I am sorry for my sin." When a brother says, "God has forgiven me. Will you forgive?" clasp his hand, and say, "As I hope to be forgiven, I forgive.". . . When the enemy is seeking in every way to destroy, shall church members unite with him to discourage a man who is repentant, and is asking for forgiveness?[376]

Love is unsuspecting, ever placing the most favorable construction upon the motives and acts of others. Love will never needlessly expose the faults of others. It does not listen eagerly to unfavorable reports, but rather seeks to bring to mind some good qualities of the one defamed.[377]

Self-Condemnation

It is the one whose conscience condemns him that so readily passes judgment. Let everyone tremble and be afraid of himself. Let him see that his own heart is right with God. Let him weed his own garden; he will find enough to keep him busily employed. If he does this work faithfully, he will not have time to find fault with the gardens of others.[378] The very act of looking for evil in others develops defects in those who look. These would be alarmed could they see the facts that are registered against them in the books of Heaven.

The man with the beam in his own eye thinks he has discovered a mote in his brother's eye. But the very discovery of the mote is the sign of the beam.[379]

The effort to earn salvation by one's own works inevitably leads men to pile up human exactions as a barrier against sin. For, seeing that they fail to keep the law, they will devise rules and regulations of their own to force themselves to obey. All this turns the mind away from God to self. His love dies out of the heart, and with it perishes love for his fellow men. A system of human invention, with its multitudinous exactions, will lead its advocates to judge all who come short of the prescribed human standard. The atmosphere of selfish and narrow criticism stifles the noble and generous emotions, and causes men to become self-centered judges and petty spies.

The Pharisees were of this class. They came forth from their religious services, not humbled with a sense of their own weakness, not grateful for the great privileges that God had given them. They came forth filled with spiritual pride, and their theme was, "Myself, my feelings, my knowledge, my ways." Their own attainments became the standard by which they judged others. Putting on the robes of self-dignity, they mounted the judgment seat to criticize and condemn.[380] There is a great variety of ways of deceiving self; and one of the most ruinous ways to cripple our usefulness is to cultivate evilspeaking and criticism of others. Those who have done this must be humble their hearts before God, and instead of denouncing others, must pro-

---

376–*Reflecting Christ*, p. 203.
377–*The Signs of the Times*, February 1, 1883.
378–*The Review and Herald*, October 29, 1901.

379–*The Youth's Instructor*, September 21, 1899.
380–*Thoughts From the Mount of Blessing*, p. 123.

claim against themselves.[381]

True Workers

Many have borne so few burdens, their hearts have known so little real anguish, they have felt so little perplexity and distress in behalf of others, that they cannot understand the work of the true burden-bearer. No more capable are they of appreciating his burdens than is the child of understanding the care and toil of his burdened father. The child may wonder at his father's fears and perplexities. These appear needless to him. But when years of experience shall have been added to his life, when he himself comes to bear its burdens, he will look back upon his father's life, and understand that which was once so incomprehensible. Bitter experience has given him knowledge.

The work of many a burden-bearer is not understood, his labors are not appreciated, until death lays him low. When others take up the burdens he has laid down, and meet the difficulties he encountered, they can understand how his faith and courage were tested. Often then the mistakes they were so quick to censure are lost sight of. Experience teaches them sympathy. God permits men to be placed in positions of responsibility. When they err, He has power to correct or to remove them. We should be careful not to take into our hands the work of judging that belongs to God.[382] O, how can Christians afford to speak words of criticism and faultfinding,— words that stir up the worst passions of the human heart? The talent of speech is too precious a gift to be abused in this way. Let us refrain from uttering any words that would stir up a spirit of antagonism or retaliation. When irritated, let us remain silent.[383]

Inexcusable

Much is involved in the matter of judging. Remember that soon your life record will pass in review before God. Remember, too, that He has said: "Thou art inexcusable, O man, whosoever thou art that judgest: for wherein thou judgest another, thou condemnest thyself; for thou that judgest doest the same things. But we are sure that the judgment of God is according to truth against them which commit such things. And thinkest thou this, O man, that judgest them which do such things, and doest the same, that thou shalt escape the judgment of God?" Romans 2:1–3. . . .

Earnest workers have no time to dwell upon the defects of others. They behold the Saviour, and by beholding become changed into His likeness. He is the One Whose example we are to follow in our character building. In His life upon the Earth He plainly revealed the divine nature. We should strive to be perfect in our sphere, as He was perfect in His sphere.[384]

To the accusing Pharisees Christ said: "He that is without sin among you, let him first cast a stone." John 8:7. There are those who are premature in their desire to reform things that to them appear faulty. They think that they should be chosen to take the place of

---

381–*The Review and Herald*, August 16, 1892.
382–*Gospel Workers*, pp. 473, 474.

383–*The Review and Herald*, September 20, 1906.
384–*Testimonies for the Church*, vol. 8, pp. 85, 86.

those who have made mistakes. They undervalue what these workers have done while others were looking on and criticizing. By their actions they say: "I can do great things. I can carry the work forward successfully." To those who think they know so well how to avoid mistakes, I am instructed to say: "Judge not, that ye be not judged." Matthew 7:1. You might avoid mistakes on some points, but on other things you are liable to make grave blunders, which would be very difficult to remedy and which would bring confusion into the work. These mistakes might do more harm than those your brethren have made.[385]

The Lord wants His people to follow other methods than that of condemning wrong, even though the condemnation be just. He wants us to do something more than to hurl at our adversaries charges that only drive them further from the truth. The work which Christ came to do in our world was not to erect barriers and constantly thrust upon the people the fact that they were wrong.[386]

When we condemn or criticize others, we declare ourselves guilty; in the very act of judging them, we are breaking God's law. Our own character is revealed in the way we treat others. He who is censorious, self-sufficient, in judging others, shows that he himself is devoid of the grace of Christ. It is those that are blinded by the enemy to their own defects of character who are forward in criticizing and condemning. Their own lack of the spirit of forbearance and love leads them to make a world of an atom.

He who is watching for the defects of others, ready to accuse and condemn, is doing the same work in which Satan has been engaged since his rebellion. He links himself with him who is the accuser of the brethren.

Thus in accusing others we are passing sentence upon ourselves, and God declares that this sentence shall stand. Remember this, you who are so ready to criticize others. The sentence which you think to pass upon them you are passing upon yourselves, and thus it stands in the records of Heaven. God accepts the sentence, your own verdict against yourselves. Are you willing to abide by it in the final day?[387] God will charge those who unwisely expose the mistakes of their brethren with sin of far greater magnitude than He will charge the one who makes a misstep. Criticism and condemnation of the brethren are counted as criticism and condemnation of Christ.[388]

Clear Vision

If we imagine we see wrong in our brother, let us not judge him; let us not go to work secretly to make the mote appears as large as possible before others, depreciating our brother by secret whisperings when he knows nothing of our suspicious and evil thoughts. How cruel it is to judge, condemn, and pass sentence upon your brother when he has not the slightest suspicion that you are not his friend. It was in this secret manner that Satan carried on his work in Heaven, and now through human

---

385–*Testimonies for the Church*, vol. 7, pp. 278, 279.
386–*Testimonies for the Church*, vol. 6, p. 121.

387–*The Signs of the Times*, March 21, 1892.
388–*Selected Messages*, book 3, p. 345.

agencies who submit to his control, he carries on the same hypocritical course of action.[389]

Not until you feel that you could sacrifice your own self-dignity, and even lay down your life in order to save an erring brother, have you cast the beam out of your own eye so that you are prepared to help your brother. Then you can approach him and touch his heart. No one has ever been reclaimed from a wrong position by censure and reproach; but many have thus been driven from Christ and led to seal their hearts against conviction.[390]

To speak the Word of God with faithfulness is a work of the greatest importance. But this is an entirely different work from continually censuring, thinking evil, and drawing apart from one another. Judging and reproving are two different things. God has laid upon His servants the work of reproving in love those who err; but He has forbidden and denounced the thoughtless judging so common among professed believers.

Actions speak louder than words, and those who draw from their brethren show plainly that they do not wish to work with them, that they surmise evil of the men to whom the Lord has given a place in His work.

Those who show this lack of faith and confidence in their brethren grieve the Spirit of God. The Lord calls upon us to put away all haughtiness, to manifest sincere sympathy for the erring, who are seeking to recover themselves from the snare of the enemy.[391]

If, after one has done the best he can in his judgment, another thinks he can see where he could have improved the matter, he should kindly and patiently give the brother the benefit of his judgment, but should not censure him nor question his integrity of purpose any sooner than he himself would wish to be suspected or unjustly censured. If the brother who feels the cause of God at heart sees that, in his earnest efforts to do, he has made a failure, he will feel deeply over the matter; for he will be inclined to distrust himself and to lose confidence in his own judgment. Nothing will so weaken his courage and godlike manhood as to realize his mistakes in the work that God has appointed him to do, a work which he loves better than his life. How unjust, then, for his brethren who discover his errors to keep pressing the thorn deeper and deeper into his heart, to make him feel more intensely, when with every thrust they are weakening his faith and courage, and his confidence in himself to work successfully in the upbuilding of the cause of God.

Pitying Tenderness

Frequently the truth and facts are to be plainly spoken to the erring, to make them see and feel their error that they may reform. But this should ever be done with pitying tenderness, not with harshness or severity, but considering one's own weakness, lest he also be tempted. When the one at fault sees and acknowledges his error, then, instead of grieving him, and seeking to make him feel more deeply, comfort should be given. In the sermon

---

389–*The Review and Herald*, August 16, 1892.
390–*Thoughts From the Mount of Blessing*, pp. 128, 129.

391–*The Review and Herald*, October 29, 1901.

of Christ upon the mount He said: "Judge not, that ye be not judged. For with what judgment ye judge, ye shall be judged: and with what measure ye mete, it shall be measured to you again." [Matthew 7:1, 2.] Our Saviour reproved for rash judgment. "Why beholdest thou the mote that is in thy brother's eye; ... and, behold, a beam is in thine own eye?" [Verses 3, 4.] It is frequently the case that while one is quick to discern the errors of his brethren, he may be in greater faults himself, but be blind to them.[392]

Do not think yourself better than other men, and set yourself up as their judge. Since you cannot discern motive, you are incapable of judging another. In criticizing him, you are passing sentence upon yourself; for you show that you are a participant with Satan, the accuser of the brethren. The Lord says, "Examine yourselves, whether ye be in the faith; prove your own selves." This is our work. "If we would judge ourselves, we should not be judged." 2 Corinthians 13:5; 1 Corinthians 11:31.[393] Instead of judging our brethren, let us judge ourselves. Let us make sure that we are among the number who are "elect according to the foreknowledge of God the Father, through sanctification of the Spirit, unto obedience and sprinkling of the blood of Jesus Christ." "Seeing ye have purified your souls in obeying the truth through the Spirit unto unfeigned love of the brethren, see that ye love one another with a pure heart fervently." [1 Peter 1:2, 22.][394]

My brethren, the time has come for every man to examine critically his own case. The time has come for men to keep their words of faultfinding for their individual selves. Let those who have been free to express their ideas regarding the error of their brother's course, examine their own lives by the light of the Word of God. There is a great work of reconversion to be done before the way for the Lord's coming shall be prepared. Men and women who have long professed to serve the Lord need to experience the quickening power of the Holy Spirit.[395]

There are times when we have to take a decided stand, but, in magnifying the Lord, be sure that you do not condemn and make charges against others. It would cause all the powers of Hell to rejoice if our people were to become divided. The way has been preparing for contention and division. Some are in great danger of drifting into infidelity. Now, let your study be to save these imperiled souls. I have sorrow, great sorrow of heart, that they do not understand their bearings.[396]

The practice of passing judgment upon others is common, indeed, it is almost universal, even among those who claim to be Christians. Many regard it as a mark of superior discernment to criticize the motives of others. But in the light of the Saviour's words it is a very serious thing thus to sit in judgment upon another. The wisdom displayed in discerning stains upon the character of others is that described by the apostle James, which "descendeth not from above, but is earthly, sensual, devilish." [James 3:15.][397]

392–*Testimonies for the Church*, vol. 3, pp. 92, 93.
393–*The Desire of Ages*, p. 314.
394–*The Review and Herald*, October 29, 1901.
395–*The Review and Herald*, November 14, 1907.
396–*Spalding and Magan Collection*, p. 383.
397–*The Signs of the Times*, March 14, 1892.

Self-Examination

The Lord is not pleased with His people when they neglect to criticize their own soul, criticizing others instead. This is Satan's work. When you do this work, remember that the enemy is using you as a means of tempting others, in order that those who should be united in harmony and joy, building up one another in the most holy faith, shall be warring and complaining because someone else is sinning. Christ has not made you a sin-bearer. You cannot even bear your own sin. Therefore be very careful not to take up any reproach against your neighbor. God wants His people to be free.... Shall we not remember that by the words we speak we may either wound or heal? Shall we not remember that as we judge, so we shall be judged, we who perhaps have had many more opportunities than those whom we judge?

Our hearts must be melted into tenderness and love for one another. We may criticize ourselves just as severely as we please. The one who criticizes another gives evidence that he is the very one who needs to criticize himself. Pray God to show you what you must remove from yourselves in order that you may see the Kingdom of God.[398]

Wheat and Tares

There are many who are treated as tares and hopeless subjects, whom Christ is drawing to Himself. Men judge from the outward appearance, and think they discern the true measurement of a man's character; but they make many blunders in their judgments. They put a high estimate upon a man whose appearance is as an angel of light, when in thought and heart he is corrupt and unworthy. On another whose appearance is not so favorable, they pass criticism, make him an offender for a word, and would separate him from the church because of his supposed defective character, when it may be that He Who reads the heart, sees true moral worth in the man. Human judgment does not decide any case; for the Lord's thoughts are not our thoughts, neither are His ways our ways. He whom we would separate from the church as altogether unworthy, is the object of the Lord's solicitude and love. All Heaven is engaged in doing the appointed work of drawing souls to God, and the Lord has said concerning His Word, "It shall not return unto Me void, but it shall accomplish that which I please, and it shall prosper in the thing whereto I sent it." [Isaiah 55:11.]

Then since the Lord is working through His Own divine agency upon the hearts of those whom we would term hopeless subjects, let not man be officious, let him stand out of the way of God's work; for His Word that goeth forth from His mouth, will accomplish its appointed work, and prosper in the thing whereunto it is sent. Let not man set himself up as judge of his brethren; for God "hath appointed a day in the which He will judge the world in righteousness by that Man Whom He hath ordained; whereof He hath given assurance unto all men, in that He hath raised Him from the dead." [Acts 17:31.][399]

398–*Our High Calling*, p. 233.

399–*The Review and Herald*, January 3, 1893

Disunion

If there is disunion among those who claim to believe the truth, the world will conclude that this people cannot be of God, because they are working against one another. When we are one with Christ, we shall be united among ourselves. Those who are not yoked up with Christ always pull the wrong way. They possess a temperament that belongs to man's carnal nature, and at the least excuse passion is wide-awake to meet passion. This causes a collision; and loud voices are heard in committee meetings, in board meetings, and in public assemblies, opposing reform methods.[400]

Satan exults over the condition of God's professed people. While many are neglecting their own souls, they eagerly watch for an opportunity to criticize and condemn others. All have defects of character, and it is not hard to find something that jealousy can interpret to their injury. "Now," say these self-constituted judges, "we have facts. We will fasten upon them an accusation from which they cannot clear themselves." They wait for a fitting opportunity and then produce their bundle of gossip and bring forth their tidbits.[401] The powers of darkness will assault every soul, but let us not join with the evil one in his work, and deal with severity to discourage and dishearten the weak and erring. Let us be pitiful, compassionate one to another, and let an influence go out from us to heal, to bind up, to establish, rather than to wound and to uproot.[402]

All should take heed to the words of our Saviour: "A good man out of the good treasure of the heart bringeth forth good things: and an evil man out of the evil treasure bringeth forth evil things. But I say unto you, That every idle word that men shall speak, they shall give account thereof in the day of Judgment. For by thy words thou shalt be justified, and by thy words thou shalt be condemned." [Matthew 12:35–37.] How little regard is paid even to the instructions of the heavenly Teacher. Many either do not study the Word of God or do not heed its solemn truths, and these plain truths will rise up in Judgment and condemn them.[403] God is the embodiment of benevolence, mercy, and love. Those who are truly connected with Him cannot be at variance with one another. His Spirit ruling in the heart will create harmony, love, and unity. The opposite of this is seen among the children of Satan. It is his work to stir up envy, strife, and jealousy. In the name of my Master I ask the professed followers of Christ: What fruit do you bear?[404]

Severity and faultfinding must be rebuked as the workings of Satan. Mutual love and confidence must be encouraged and strengthened in the members of the church. Let all, in the fear of God and with love to their brethren, close their ears to gossip and censure. Direct the talebearer to the teachings of God's Word. Bid him obey the Scriptures and carry his complaints directly to those whom he thinks in error. This united action would bring a flood of light into

---

400–*Testimonies for the Church*, vol. 6, pp. 139, 140.
401–*Testimonies for the Church*, vol. 5, p. 94.
402–*The Review and Herald*, October 24, 1893.
403–*Testimonies for the Church*, vol. 1, pp. 499, 500.
404–*Testimonies for the Church*, vol. 5, p. 28.

the church and close the door to a flood of evil. Thus God would be glorified, and many souls would be saved.[405]

How much evil is done by unwise condemnation of others. O, whatever we do, let us not interpose ourselves between souls and God. How often has criticism of others, in the church or in the world, resulted in closing the door by which most precious truths might have found an entrance to hearts, and souls might have been converted to God. We need to humble ourselves at every step, and lift up the Man of Calvary, the Lamb of God that taketh away the sin of the world. Talk of the loveliness of the character of Christ. We are charged to be "holy in all manner of conversation." [1 Peter 1:15.][406]

Ungenerous, unchristian expressions of judgment, of criticism, of condemnation of others, if not repented of, will sink the soul in ruin. The piety of the man who thus condemns others, is measured by the hidden motives, the secret plans and plottings of evil against those with whom he is at enmity. The value of his conduct, the real influence of his life, is summed up as wanting by the Lord of Heaven, Who reads the secrets of every soul. That spoken in the ear, in the closet, will be proclaimed upon the housetop. No man can fully know the measure of the good or evil of his course of action, because the Lord holds in His Own hands the consequences of our deeds. The Lord permits circumstances to arise that will bring into notice the good qualities of one who is suspected of wrong. The Lord will permit persons to pass through strait places, where the surroundings will work to develop the traits of character that are condemned by Christ. The evil work that evil workers intended to do will not bring about the results they had designed; for the Lord will manage the matter so that good will be brought out of evil. But no credit or reward will be given to him who purposed to do harm to the purchase of the blood of Christ, even though good resulted from his plottings of evil. The Lord set counter-agencies to work to preserve His people from being deceived and injured.[407]

Is there no law of kindness to be observed? Have Christians been authorized of God to criticize and condemn one another? Is it honorable, or even honest, to win from the lips of another, under the guise of friendship, secrets which have been entrusted to him, and then turn the knowledge thus gained to his injury? Is it Christian charity to gather up every floating report, to unearth everything that will cast suspicion on the character of another, and then take delight in using it to injure him? Satan exults when he can defame or wound a follower of Christ. He is "the accuser of our brethren." [Revelation 12:10.] Shall Christians aid him in his work?[408]

A Form of Godliness

We must pray more, and talk less. Iniquity abounds, and the people must be taught not to be satisfied with a form of godliness without the spirit and power. If we are intent upon searching our own

---

405–*Testimonies for the Church*, vol. 5, pp. 609, 610.
406–*The Review and Herald*, April 26, 1892

407–*The Review and Herald*, August 16, 1892.
408–*Testimonies for the Church*, vol. 5, p. 95.

hearts, putting away our sins, and correcting our evil tendencies, our souls will not be lifted up unto vanity; we shall be distrustful of ourselves, having an abiding sense that our sufficiency is of God.

We have far more to fear from within than from without. The hindrances to strength and success are far greater from the church itself than from the world. Unbelievers have a right to expect that those who profess to be keeping the commandments of God and the faith of Jesus, will do more than any other class to promote and honor, by their consistent lives, by their godly example and their active influence, the cause which they represent.[409]

It is not the opposition of the world that most endangers the church of Christ. It is the evil cherished in the hearts of believers that works their most grievous disaster and most surely retards the progress of God's cause. There is no surer way of weakening spirituality than by cherishing envy, suspicion, faultfinding, and evil surmising. On the other hand, the strongest witness that God has sent His Son into the world is the existence of harmony and union among men of varied dispositions who form His church. This witness it is the privilege of the followers of Christ to bear. But in order to do this, they must place themselves under Christ's command. Their characters must be conformed to His character and their wills to His will.[410]

Restitution

If we have in any manner defrauded or injured our brother, we should make restitution. If we have unwittingly borne false witness, if we have misstated his words, if we have injured his influence in any way, we should go to the ones with whom we have conversed about him, and take back all our injurious misstatements.[411]

Nearing the End

As the people of God approach the perils of the last days, Satan holds earnest consultation with his angels as to the most successful plan of overthrowing their faith…. "We must cause distraction and division. We must destroy their anxiety for their own souls, and lead them to criticize, to judge, and to accuse and condemn one another, and to cherish selfishness and enmity. For these sins, God banished us from His presence; and all who follow our example will meet a similar fate."[412]

We are nearing the end of time. Trials will be abundant from without, but let them not come from within the church. Let God's professed people deny self for the truth's sake, for Christ's sake. "For we must all appear before the judgment seat of Christ; that everyone may receive the things done in his body, according to that he hath done, whether it be good or bad." [2 Corinthians 5:10.] Everyone who truly loves God will have the Spirit of Christ and a fervent love for his brethren. The more a person's

---

409–*The Review and Herald*, March 22, 1887.
410–*The Acts of the Apostles*, p. 549.

411–*Thoughts From the Mount of Blessing*, p. 59.
412–*The Spirit of Prophecy*, vol. 4, pp. 337–340.

heart is in communion with God, and the more his affections are centered in Christ, the less will he be disturbed by the roughness and hardships he meets in this life. Those who are growing up to the full stature of men and women in Christ Jesus, will become more and more like Christ in character, rising above the disposition to murmur and be discontented. They will despise to be faultfinders.[413] [Christ] declared that the spirit of criticism, of judging one another, is a source of weakness in the church today. Things are spoken that should never find utterance. Everyone who by word of mouth places an obstruction in the way of a fellow Christian, has an account to settle with God.

Character

With earnest solemnity [He] declared: "The church is made up of many minds, each of whom has an individuality. I gave My life in order that men and women, by divine grace, might blend in revealing a perfect pattern of My character, while at the same time retaining their individuality. No one has the right to disparage the individuality of any other human mind, by uttering words of criticism and faultfinding and condemnation."[414]

Character is being weighed in the balances of the sanctuary, and it should be the earnest desire of all to walk humbly and carefully, lest, neglecting to let their light shine forth to the world, they fail of the grace of God and lose everything that is valuable. All dissension, all differences and faultfinding, should be put away, with all evil speaking and bitterness; kindness, love, and compassion for one another should be cherished, that the prayer of Christ that His disciples might be one as He is One with the Father may be answered. The harmony and unity of the church are the credentials that they present to the world that Jesus is the Son of God. Genuine conversion will ever lead to genuine love for Jesus and for all those for whom He died.[415]

413–*Testimonies for the Church*, vol. 5, pp. 483, 484.

414–*The Signs of the Times*, September 20, 1906.
415–*Testimonies for the Church*, vol. 5, p. 279.

Chapter 16

The Cleansing

The Wedding Garment

"Then saith he to his servants, 'The wedding is ready, but they which were bidden were not worthy. Go ye therefore into the highways, and as many as ye shall find, bid to the marriage.' So those servants went out into the highways, and gathered together all as many as they found, both bad and good: and the wedding was furnished with guests.

"And when the king came in to see the guests, he saw there a man which had not on a wedding garment: And he saith unto him, Friend, how camest thou in hither not having a wedding garment? And he was speechless. Then said the king to the servants, 'Bind him hand and foot, and take him away, and cast him into outer darkness; there shall be weeping and gnashing of teeth.'"[416]

By the king's examination of the guests at the feast is represented a work of Judgment. The guests at the Gospel feast are those who profess to serve God, those whose names are written in the Book of Life. But not all who profess to be Christians are true disciples. Before the final reward is given, it must be decided who are fitted to share the inheritance of the righteous.[417]

Only the covering which Christ Himself has provided can make us meet to appear in God's presence. This covering, the robe of His Own righteousness, Christ will put upon every repenting, believing soul. "I counsel thee," He says, "to buy of Me ... white raiment, that thou mayest be clothed, and that the shame of thy nakedness do not appear." Revelation 3:18.

This robe, woven in the loom of Heaven, has in it not one thread of human devising. Christ in His humanity wrought out a perfect character, and this character He offers to impart to us.... Everything that we of ourselves can do is defiled by sin. But the Son of God "was manifested to take away our sins; and in Him is no sin." [1 John 3:5] ... By His

---

416–Matthew 22:8–13.

417–*Christ's Object Lessons*, p. 310.

perfect obedience He has made it possible for every human being to obey God's commandments. When we submit ourselves to Christ, the heart is united with His heart, the will is merged in His will, the mind becomes one with His mind, the thoughts are brought into captivity to Him; we live His life.[418] This testimony must work deep repentance, and all that truly receive it will obey it and be purified.[419] Unless [we] trust in the righteousness of Christ as [our] only security; unless [we] copy His character, labor in His Spirit, [we] are naked, [we] have not on the robe of His righteousness.[420]

The Day of Atonement

We are living in the solemn hour of the Judgment, when we should afflict our souls, confess our errors, repent of our sins, and pray one for another that we may be healed.[421] The typical Day of Atonement ... was a special season of great humiliation and confession of sins before God. The antitypical Day of Atonement is to be of the same character.[422] The subject of the sanctuary and the investigative Judgment should be clearly understood by the people of God. All need a knowledge for themselves of the position and work of their great High Priest. Otherwise it will be impossible for them to exercise the faith which is essential at this time or to occupy the position which God designs them to fill.[423]

At the time appointed for the Judgment—the close of the 2,300 days, in 1844—began the work of investigation and blotting out of sins.... Both the living and the dead are to be judged "out of those things which were written in the books, according to their works." [Revelation 20:12].[424] We cannot afford to delay this work of confession and humbling of soul, that our offerings may be acceptable unto God.[425] Now is the time when we are to confess and forsake our sins that they may go beforehand to Judgment and be blotted out.[426]

The religion of Christ means more than the forgiveness of sin; it means taking away our sins, and filling the vacuum with the graces of the Holy Spirit.... It means a heart emptied of self, and blessed with the abiding presence of Christ.[427] The work of the investigative Judgment and the blotting out of sins is to be accomplished before the Second Advent of the Lord.[428] What we make of ourselves in probationary time, that we must remain to all eternity. Death brings dissolution to the body, but makes no change in the character. The coming of Christ does not change our characters; it only fixes them forever beyond all change.[429]

Like Him in Character

[Jesus] rejoiced in the consciousness that He could and would do more

---

418–*Christ's Object Lessons*, pp. 311, 312.
419–*Testimonies for the Church,* vol. 1, p. 181.
420–*The Review and Herald*, January 17, 1893.
421–*The Review and Herald*, May 13, 1884.
422–*Testimonies for the Church*, vol. 5, p. 520.
423–*The Great Controversy*, p. 488.

424–*The Great Controversy*, p. 486.
425–*My Life Today*, p. 348.
426–*In Heavenly Places*, p. 348.
427–*Christ's Object Lessons*, pp. 419, 420.
428–*The Great Controversy*, p. 485.
429–*Testimonies for the Church*, vol. 5, p. 466.

for His followers than He had promised; that from Him would flow forth love and compassion, cleansing the soul temple, and making men like Him in character....[430] We must empty the soul temple of every defilement, and let the Spirit of God take full possession of the heart, that the character may be transformed.[431] Are we awake to the work that is going on in the heavenly sanctuary, or are we waiting for some compelling power to come upon the church before we shall arouse?[432] Christ is cleansing the temple in Heaven from the sins of the people, and we must work in harmony with him upon the Earth, cleansing the soul temple from its moral defilement.[433] Now, while our great High Priest is making the atonement for us, we should seek to become perfect in Christ.[434]

In order to receive God's help, man must realize his weakness and deficiency; he must apply his own mind to the great change to be wrought in himself; he must be aroused to earnest and persevering prayer and effort.[435] We must take time to pray. If we allow our minds to be absorbed by worldly interests, the Lord may give us time by removing from us our idols of gold, of houses, or of fertile lands.[436] We must enter upon the work individually. We must pray more, and talk less. Iniquity abounds, and the people must be taught not to be satisfied with a form of godliness without the Spirit and power.[437] All who would have their names retained in the Book of Life should now, in the few remaining days of their probation, afflict their souls before God by sorrow for sin and true repentance. There must be deep, faithful searching of heart.[438] "The Lord is very pitiful, and of tender mercy." [James 5:11.] ... There is no chapter in our experience too dark for Him to read; there is no perplexity too difficult for Him to unravel. None have fallen so low, none are so vile, that they cannot find deliverance in Christ.... No cry from a soul in need is unheeded.[439]

Freedom

"The Spirit of the Lord God is upon me; because the Lord hath anointed me ... to proclaim liberty to the captives, and the opening of the prison to them that are bound; to proclaim the acceptable year of the Lord, ... to appoint unto them that mourn in Zion, to give unto them ... the garment of praise for the spirit of heaviness; that they might be called Trees of Righteousness, The Planting of the Lord, that He might be glorified."[440]

In ancient times criminals were sometimes sold into slavery by the judges; in some cases, debtors were sold by their creditors; and poverty even led persons to sell themselves or their children.[441] "And if thy brother that dwelleth by thee be waxen poor, and be sold unto thee; thou shalt not compel him to serve

---

430–*The Acts of the Apostles*, p. 23
431–*The Review and Herald*, May 28, 1889.
432–*Selected Messages*, book 2, p. 122.
433–*The Review and Herald*, February 11, 1890.
434–*The Great Controversy*, p. 623.
435–*Patriarchs and Prophets*, p. 248.
436–*The Great Controversy*, p. 622.

437–*Selected Messages*, book 2, p. 122.
438–*The Great Controversy*, pp. 489, 490.
439–*The Signs of the Times*, June 18, 1902.
440–Isaiah 61:1–3.
441–*Patriarchs and Prophets*, p. 310.

as a bondservant: But as an hired servant, and as a sojourner, he shall be with thee, and shall serve thee unto the year of jubilee."[442] Man sold himself to Satan, but Jesus bought back the race, redeeming men and women from the slavery of a cruel tyrant.[443]

"And ye shall hallow the fiftieth year, and proclaim liberty throughout all the land unto all the inhabitants thereof: it shall be a jubilee unto you; and ye shall return every man unto his possession, and ye shall return every man unto his family."[444] "On the tenth day of the seventh month, in the Day of Atonement,"[Leviticus 25:9] the trumpet of the jubilee was sounded. Throughout the land, wherever the Jewish people dwelt, the sound was heard, calling upon all the children of Jacob to welcome the year of release. On the great Day of Atonement satisfaction was made for the sins of Israel, and with gladness of heart the people would welcome the jubilee.

As in the sabbatical year, the land was not to be sown or reaped, and all that it produced was to be regarded as the rightful property of the poor. Certain classes of Hebrew slaves—all who did not receive their liberty in the sabbatical year—were now set free. But that which especially distinguished the year of jubilee was the reversion of all landed property to the family of the original possessor.[445]

A Pure Heart

"Who shall ascend into the hill of the Lord? or who shall stand in His holy place? He that hath clean hands, and a pure heart."[446] I saw that God ... enjoins upon His people in the latter day strict cleanliness of body and clothing and purity of mind, of thoughts, and of words, for He is to translate them to Heaven.[447] The Lord has shown me the danger of letting our minds be filled with worldly thoughts and cares.... For if the mind is filled with other things, present truth is shut out, and there is no place in our foreheads for the seal of the living God.[448] The mind is befogged by sensual malaria. The thoughts need purifying.[449] If the thoughts are wrong, the feelings will be wrong; and the thoughts and feelings combined make up the moral character.[450]

This is the fitting up place to appear in His presence.[451] It is in this life that we are to separate sin from us, through faith in the atoning blood of Christ.[452] "On that day shall the priest make an atonement for you, to cleanse you, that ye may be clean from all your sins before the Lord."[453] "Be not conformed to this world: but be ye transformed by the renewing of your mind, that ye may prove what is that good, and acceptable, and perfect, will of God."[454] "For the weapons of our warfare

---

442–Leviticus 25:39, 40.
443–*The Bible Echo*, October 15, 1900.
444–Leviticus 25:10.
445–*Patriarchs and Prophets*, pp. 533, 534.

446–Psalm 24:3, 4.
447–*Manuscript Releases*, vol. 21, p. 375.
448–*Early Writings*, p. 58.
449–Letter 139, 1898.
450–*In Heavenly Places*, p. 164.
451–*Spiritual Gifts*, vol. 2, p. 226.
452–*The Great Controversy*, p. 623.
453–Leviticus 16:30.
454–Romans 12:2.

are not of the flesh, but mighty before God to the casting down of strongholds, casting down imaginations, and every high thing that is exalted against the knowledge of God, and bringing every thought into captivity to the obedience of Christ."[455]

The law requires that the soul itself be pure and the mind holy, that the thoughts and feelings may be in accordance with the standard of love and righteousness.[456] Every act is judged by the motives that prompt it.[457] God's law reaches the feelings and motives, as well as the outward acts.... The books of Heaven record the sins that would have been committed had there been opportunity.[458] The law of God takes note of the jealousy, envy, hatred, malignity, revenge, lust, and ambition that surge through the soul, but have not found expression in outward action, because the opportunity, not the will, has been wanting.[459] God will bring every work into Judgment, with every secret thing.[460] For our present and eternal good, let us criticize our actions, to see how they stand in the light of the law of God.[461] Now is the time for the law of God to be in our minds, foreheads, and written in our hearts.[462]

The Books

God has an exact record of every unjust account and every unfair dealing.... He makes no mistakes in His estimation of character.[463] Could the veil which separates the visible from the invisible world be swept back, ... the children of men [would see] an angel recording every word and deed, which they must meet again in the Judgment.[464] Every word uttered, every departure from integrity, every action that sullies the soul, will be weighed in the balances of the sanctuary.... The mind will recall all the thoughts and acts of the past; the whole life will come in review like the scenes in a panorama.[465] As the books of record are opened in the Judgment, the lives of all who have believed on Jesus come in review before God. Beginning with those who first lived upon the Earth, our Advocate presents the cases of each successive generation, and closes with the living. Every name is mentioned, every case closely investigated.... When any have sins remaining upon the books of record, unrepented of and unforgiven, their names will be blotted out of the book of God's remembrance.[466]

Make the Effort

I was shown that if God's people make no efforts on their part, but wait for the refreshing to come upon them and remove their wrongs and correct their errors; if they depend upon that to cleanse them from filthiness of the flesh and spirit, and fit them to engage in the loud cry of the third angel, they will be

---

455–2 Corinthians 10:4, 5.
456–*Selected Messages*, book 1, p. 211.
457–*Christ's Object Lessons*, p. 316.
458–*The Signs of the Times*, July 31, 1901.
459–*The Signs of the Times*, April 15, 1886.
460–*The Signs of the Times*, July 31, 1901.
461–Letter 22, 1901.
462–*Early Writings*, p. 57.

463–*The Great Controversy*, p. 486.
464–*The Great Controversy*, p. 487.
465–*The Review and Herald*, November 4, 1884.
466–*The Great Controversy*, p. 483.

found wanting.[467] Let no one say, I cannot remedy my defects of character; for if you come to this decision, you will certainly fail to obtain everlasting life. The impossibility lies in your own will. If you will not, then you cannot overcome. The real difficulty arises from the corruption of unsanctified hearts, and an unwillingness to submit to the control of God.[468]

"He that covereth his sins shall not prosper: but whoso confesseth and forsaketh them shall have mercy."[469] "But if we walk in the light, as He is in the light, we have fellowship one with another, and the blood of Jesus Christ His Son cleanseth us from all sin. If we say that we have no sin, we deceive ourselves, and the truth is not in us. If we confess our sins, He is faithful and just to forgive us our sins, and to cleanse us from all unrighteousness. If we say that we have not sinned, we make Him a liar, and His word is not in us."[470] Many a sin is left unconfessed, to be confronted in the day of final accounts; better far to see your sins now, to confess them, and put them away, while the atoning sacrifice pleads in your behalf.[471] Sins that have not been repented of and forsaken will not be pardoned and blotted out of the books of record, but will stand to witness against the sinner in the day of God.[472] All who endeavor to excuse or conceal their sins, and permit them to remain upon the books of Heaven, unconfessed and unforgiven, will be overcome by Satan.[473] Satan well knows that all whom he can lead to neglect prayer and the searching of the Scriptures, will be overcome by his attacks. Therefore he invents every possible device to engross the mind.[474]

Instruction in Righteousness

From the Holy of Holies, there goes on the grand work of instruction. The angels of God are communicating to men. Christ officiates in the sanctuary.... There must be a purifying of the soul here upon the Earth, in harmony with Christ's cleansing of the sanctuary in Heaven. There we shall see more clearly as we are seen. We shall know as we are known.[475] As fast as His people can bear it, the Lord reveals to them their errors in doctrine and their defects of character.[476] He reveals to man the defects that mar his life, and calls upon him to repent and turn from sin.[477] Through faith in Christ, every deficiency of character may be supplied, every defilement cleansed, every fault corrected, every excellence developed.[478]

By a close scrutiny of their daily life under all circumstances they would know their own motives, the principles which actuate them. This daily review of our acts, to see whether conscience approves or condemns, is necessary for all who wish to arrive at the perfection

---

467–*Testimonies for the Church*, vol. 1, p. 619.
468–*The Youth's Instructor*, January 28, 1897.
469–Proverbs 28:13.
470–1 John 1:7–10.
471–*The Review and Herald*, November 28, 1893.
472–*The Great Controversy*, p. 486.

473–*Patriarchs and Prophets*, p. 202.
474–*The Great Controversy*, p. 519.
475–*The Ellen G. White 1888 Materials*, p. 27.
476–*The Spirit of Prophecy*, vol. 4, p. 186.
477–*The Signs of the Times*, July 31, 1901.
478–*Education*, p. 257.

of Christian character.[479] This is at times a very painful and discouraging work; because, as we see the deformities in our character, we keep looking at them, when we should look to Jesus and put on the robe of His righteousness.[480]

Clear Eyes

"Anoint thine eyes with eyesalve, that thou mayest see."[481] "The light of the body is the eye: if therefore thine eye be single, thy whole body shall be full of light."[482] The eye is the sensitive conscience, the inner light, of the mind. Upon its correct view of things the spiritual healthfulness of the whole soul and being depends. The "eyesalve," the Word of God, makes the conscience smart under its application; for it convicts of sin. But the smarting is necessary that the healing may follow, and the eye be single to the glory of God. The sinner, beholding himself in God's great moral looking glass, sees himself as God views him, and exercises repentance toward God and faith toward our Lord Jesus Christ. . . .

He does not leave His tempted ones with eyes that are nearly blind to their own imperfections. The man who uses the eyesalve is enabled to see himself as he is. His wretchedness is discovered; he feels his imperfections, his spiritual poverty, and his need of being healed of his spiritual malady. . . .[483] We shall not renounce sin unless we see its sinfulness; until we turn away from it in heart, there will be no real change in the life.[484]

When the light shines, making manifest and reproving the errors that were undiscovered, there must be a corresponding change in the life and character. The mistakes that are the natural result of blindness of mind are, when pointed out, no longer sins of ignorance or errors of judgment; but unless there are decided reforms in accordance with the light given, they then become presumptuous sins. The moral darkness that surrounds you will become more dense; your heart will become harder and harder, and you will be more offensive in the sight of God.[485]

The Gift of Repentance

It is the virtue that goes forth from Christ, that leads to genuine repentance. Peter made the matter clear in his statement to the Israelites when he said, "Him hath God exalted with His right hand to be a Prince and a Saviour, for to give repentance to Israel, and forgiveness of sins." Acts 5:31. We can no more repent without the Spirit of Christ to awaken the conscience than we can be pardoned without Christ. . . .

He is the only One that can implant in the heart enmity against sin. Every desire for truth and purity, every conviction of our own sinfulness, is an evidence that His Spirit is moving upon our hearts. . . .

As we behold the Lamb of God upon the cross of Calvary, the mystery

---

479–*Testimonies for the Church*, vol. 2, p. 512.
480–*Testimonies for the Church*, vol. 9, p. 182.
481–Revelation 3:18.
482–Matthew 6:22.
483–*The Review and Herald*, November 23, 1897.
484–*Steps to Christ*, p. 23.
485–*Testimonies for the Church*, vol. 5, pp. 435, 436.

of redemption begins to unfold to our minds and the goodness of God leads us to repentance. In dying for sinners, Christ manifested a love that is incomprehensible; and as the sinner beholds this love, it softens the heart, impresses the mind, and inspires contrition in the soul.[486]

The Expulsion of Sin

In the divine arrangement God does nothing without the cooperation of man. He compels no man's will. That must be given to the Lord completely, else the Lord is not able to accomplish His divine work that He would do through the human agency.[487] Under the influence of the Spirit of God, man is left free to choose whom he will serve. In the change that takes place when the soul surrenders to Christ, there is the highest sense of freedom. The expulsion of sin is the act of the soul itself. True, we have no power to free ourselves from Satan's control; but when we desire to be set free from sin, and in our great need cry out for a power out of and above ourselves, the powers of the soul are imbued with the divine energy of the Holy Spirit, and they obey the dictates of the will in fulfilling the will of God.[488]

Confession

Sin of a private character is to be confessed to Christ, the only Mediator between God and man.... Every open sin should be as openly confessed. Wrong done to a fellow being should be made right with the one who has been offended. If any ... have been guilty of evilspeaking, if they have sowed discord in the home, the neighborhood, or the church, and have stirred up alienation and dissension, if by any wrong practice they have led others into sin, these things should be confessed before God and before those who have been offended.[489] Keep nothing back from God, and neglect not the confession of your faults to the brethren when they have a connection with them. "Confess your faults one to another, and pray one for another, that ye may be healed." [James 5:16].[490]

Pray One for Another

We are to watch for souls as those that must give an account. Instead of criticizing, pray for deliverance from this evil habit; for while our time is occupied with this kind of doing, souls for whom Christ died are perishing, whom we might save.... Pray one for another that ye may be healed, and go forth to seek and to save the lost and wandering sheep. ... Christ has said, "By this shall all men know that ye are My disciples, if ye have love one to another." [John 13:35.][491] If we would offer acceptable prayer, there is a work to be done in confessing our sins to one another.[492]

"Therefore I exhort first of all that supplications, prayers, intercessions, and giving of thanks be made for all men, for kings and all who are in authority, that we may lead a quiet and peaceable life in

---

486–*Steps to Christ*, pp. 26, 27.
487–*That I May Know Him*, p. 55.
488–*The Desire of Ages*, p. 466.
489–*The Ministry of Healing*, pp. 228, 229.
490–*The Review and Herald*, November 28, 1893.
491–*The Review and Herald*, October 24, 1893.
492–*The Review and Herald*, February 9, 1897.

all godliness and reverence."[493] "We pray always for you, that our God would count you worthy of this calling, and fulfill all the good pleasure of His goodness, and the work of faith with power."[494] "The effectual fervent prayer of a righteous man availeth much."[495]

Pleading With God

Night after night, scenes have been presented to me of little companies pleading with God. He would show them some idol they had been cherishing. Some would give this up, and some would not. But the light of Heaven shone from the faces of those who would put away their idol. Then other idols would be shown to them, and again some would put these away.[496] Those who come up to every point, and stand every test, and overcome, be the price what it may, have heeded the counsel of the True Witness, and they will receive the latter rain, and thus be fitted for translation.[497] When our earthly labors are ended, and Christ shall come for His faithful children, we shall then shine forth as the sun in the kingdom of our Father. But before that time shall come, everything that is imperfect in us will have been seen and put away.[498]

Clean

"Now ye are clean through the Word which I have spoken unto you."[499] That Word must be our meat and drink. It is in this alone that the soul will find its nourishment and vitality. We must feast upon its precious instruction, that we may be renewed in the spirit of our mind, and grow up into Christ, our Living Head.[500]

"Then will I sprinkle clean water upon you, and ye shall be clean: from all your filthiness, and from all your idols, will I cleanse you. A new heart also will I give you, and a new spirit will I put within you: and I will take away the stony heart out of your flesh, and I will give you an heart of flesh."[501] "Who is a God like unto Thee. . . ? He will have compassion upon us; He will subdue our iniquities; and Thou wilt cast all their sins into the depths of the sea."[502] "I, even I, am He that blotteth out thy transgressions for Mine Own sake, and will not remember thy sins."[503] All who have truly repented of sin, and by faith claimed the blood of Christ as their atoning sacrifice, have had pardon entered against their names in the books of Heaven; as they have become partakers of the righteousness of Christ, and their characters are found to be in harmony with the law of God, their sins will be blotted out, and they themselves will be accounted worthy of eternal life.[504]

493–1 Timothy 2:1, 2.
494–2 Thessalonians 1:11.
495–James 5:16.
496–*The Upward Look*, p. 267.
497–*Testimonies for the Church*, vol. 1, p. 187.
498–*Selected Messages*, book 3, p. 427.
499–John 15:3.
500–*The Review and Herald*, November 23, 1897.
501–Ezekiel 36:25, 26.
502–Micah 7:18, 19.
503–Isaiah 43:25.
504–*The Great Controversy*, p. 483.

Prepared to Stand

In the midst of a world by its iniquity doomed to destruction, Enoch lived a life of such close communion with God that he was not permitted to fall under the power of death. The godly character of this prophet represents the state of holiness which must be attained by those who shall be "redeemed from the Earth" (Revelation 14:3) at the time of Christ's Second Advent.... Like Enoch, God's people will seek for purity of heart and conformity to His will, until they shall reflect the likeness of Christ.[505]

Not even by a thought could our Saviour be brought to yield to the power of temptation. Satan finds in human hearts some point where he can gain a foothold; some sinful desire is cherished, by means of which his temptations assert their power.... Satan could find nothing in the Son of God that would enable him to gain the victory.... This is the condition in which those must be found who shall stand in the time of trouble.[506]

The heart must be emptied of every defilement, and cleansed for the indwelling of the Spirit. It was by the confession and forsaking of sin, by earnest prayer and consecration of themselves to God, that the early disciples prepared for the outpouring of the Holy Spirit on the Day of Pentecost. The same work, only in greater degree, must be done now.[507] When the laborers have an abiding Christ in their own souls, when all selfishness is dead, when there is no rivalry, no strife for the supremacy, when oneness exists, when they sanctify themselves, so that love for one another is seen and felt, then the showers of the grace of the Holy Spirit will just as surely come upon them as that God's promise will never fail in one jot or tittle.[508] The latter rain will come, and the blessing of God will fill every soul that is purified from every defilement. It is our work today to yield our souls to Christ, that we may be fitted for the time of refreshing from the presence of the Lord—fitted for the baptism of the Holy Spirit.[509]

[Christ] is the High Priest of the church, and He has a work to do which no other can perform. By His grace He is able to keep every man from transgression.[510] "Now unto Him that is able to keep you from falling, and to present you faultless before the presence of His glory with exceeding joy, to the only wise God our Saviour, be glory and majesty, dominion and power, both now and ever. Amen."[511]

505–*Patriarchs and Prophets*, pp. 88, 89.
506–*The Great Controversy*, p. 623.
507–*The Review and Herald*, March 2, 1897.
508–*Selected Messages*, book 1, p. 175.
509–*Selected Messages*, book 1, p. 191.
510–*The Signs of the Times*, February 14, 1900.
511–Jude 24, 25.

Chapter 17

Emmanuel

Indissoluble Union

By His life and His death, Christ has achieved even more than recovery from the ruin wrought through sin. It was Satan's purpose to bring about an eternal separation between God and man; but in Christ we become more closely united to God than if we had never fallen. In taking our nature, the Saviour has bound Himself to humanity by a tie that is never to be broken. Through the eternal ages He is linked with us.... Christ is our Brother. Heaven is enshrined in humanity, and humanity is enfolded in the bosom of Infinite love.... By love's self-sacrifice, the inhabitants of Earth and Heaven are bound to their Creator in bonds of indissoluble union.[512]

One With Us

We should meditate upon the mission of Him Who came to save His people from their sins. By constantly contemplating heavenly themes, our faith and love will grow stronger.[513] Christ was treated as we deserve, that we might be treated as He deserves. He was condemned for our sins, in which He had no share, that we might be justified by His righteousness, in which we had no share. He suffered the death which was ours, that we might receive the life which was His. "With His stripes we are healed." [Isaiah 53:5.][514] In dying for sinners, Christ manifested a love that is incomprehensible; and as the sinner beholds this love, it softens the heart, impresses the mind, and inspires contrition in the soul.[515]

It would have been an almost infinite humiliation for the Son of God to take man's nature, even when Adam stood in his innocence in Eden. But Jesus accepted humanity when the race had been weakened by four thousand

---

512–*The Review and Herald*, February 25, 1915.
513–*The Review and Herald*, June 12, 1888.
514–*The Review and Herald*, February 25, 1915.
515–*Steps to Christ*, p. 27.

years of sin. Like every child of Adam He accepted the results of the working of the great law of heredity. What these results were is shown in the history of His earthly ancestors. He came with such a heredity to share our sorrows and temptations, and to give us the example of a sinless life.[516]

He was sinless, and, more than this, He was the Prince of Heaven; but in man's behalf He became sin for the race. "He was numbered with the transgressors; and He bare the sin of many, and made intercession for the transgressors." Isaiah 53:12. But what do we give up, when we give all? A sin-polluted heart, for Jesus to purify, to cleanse by His Own blood, and to save by His matchless love. And yet men think it hard to give up all! I am ashamed to hear it spoken of, ashamed to write it.[517]

He took our nature and overcame, that we through taking His nature might overcome. Made "in the likeness of sinful flesh" (Romans 8:3), He lived a sinless life.[518] He took on His sinless nature our sinful nature, that He might know how to succor them that are tempted.[519] Jesus was in all things made like unto His brethren. He became flesh, even as we are. He was hungry and thirsty and weary. He was sustained by food and refreshed by sleep. He shared the lot of man; yet He was the blameless Son of God. He was God in the flesh. His character is to be ours. The Lord says of those who believe in Him, "I will dwell in them, and walk in them; and I will be their God, and they shall be My people." 2 Corinthians 6:16.[520]

Jesus humbled Himself, clothing His Divinity with humanity, in order that He might stand as the Head and Representative of the human family, and by both precept and example condemn sin in the flesh, and give the lie to Satan's charges. He was subjected to the fiercest temptations that human nature can know, yet He sinned not; for sin is the transgression of the law. By faith He laid hold upon Divinity, even as humanity may lay hold upon infinite Power through Him.[521]

In His great love, Christ surrendered Himself for us. He gave Himself for us to meet the necessities of the striving, struggling soul. We are to surrender ourselves to Him. When this surrender is entire, Christ can finish the work He began for us by the surrender of Himself. Then He can bring to us complete restoration.[522] Through the victory of Christ the same advantages that He had are provided for man; for he may be a partaker of a Power out of and above himself, even a partaker of the divine nature, by which he may overcome the corruption that is in the world through lust.[523]

Living the Word

As we meditate upon the perfections of the Saviour, we shall desire to be wholly transformed and renewed in the image of His purity. There will be a hungering and thirsting of soul to become like Him Whom we adore. The more our

---

516–*The Desire of Ages*, p. 49.
517–*Steps to Christ*, pp. 45, 46.
518–*The Desire of Ages*, pp. 311, 312.
519–*Medical Ministry*, p. 189.

520–*The Desire of Ages*, p. 311.
521–*The Signs of the Times*, January 16, 1896.
522–*The Review and Herald*, May 30, 1907.
523–*The Signs of the Times*, January 16, 1896.

thoughts are upon Christ, the more we shall speak of Him to others and represent Him to the world.[524]

We are to live the Word, not keep it apart from our lives. The character of Christ is to be our character. We are to be transformed by the renewing of our hearts. Here is our only safety.... It is discipline of spirit, cleanness of heart and thought, that is needed.[525]

It is our privilege, by an earnest study of the Word, to learn wherein we are not manifesting the principles of that Word in our lives. And as the mirror reveals to us our defects, we are to seek by earnest prayer and faith to put them away. As we strive to meet the perfection that God requires, insensibly to us the human will become molded to the Divine. Christ's nature will be revealed in human nature; the words will become gentle and courteous, the ways kind and helpful. Though we may be largely unconscious of the change, yet the transformation is being surely wrought. Beholding day by day the glory of the Lord, we are molded into conformity to His Spirit and will.[526]

Let us give more time to the study of the Bible.[527] Fill the whole heart with the words of God. They are the living water, quenching your burning thirst. They are the living Bread from Heaven. Jesus declares, "Except ye eat the flesh of the Son of man, and drink His blood, ye have no life in you." And He explains Himself by saying, "The words that I speak unto you, they are Spirit, and they are life." John 6:53, 63. Our bodies are built up from what we eat and drink; and as in the natural economy, so in the spiritual economy: it is what we meditate upon that will give tone and strength to our spiritual nature.[528] A true believer shows that his character has been transformed by living a spiritual life, by living on every word that proceeds out of the mouth of God. His consecration is shown by the words that fall from his lips and by his zeal in good works.[529]

The Character of Christ

Perfection of character is based upon that which Christ is to us. If we have constant dependence on the merits of our Saviour, and walk in His footsteps, we shall be like Him, pure and undefiled. Our Saviour does not require impossibilities of any soul. He expects nothing of His disciples that He is not willing to give them grace and strength to perform. He would not call upon them to be perfect if He had not at His command every perfection of grace to bestow on the ones upon whom He would confer so high and holy a privilege. We are to be wholly dependent on the power that He has promised to give us. Jesus revealed no qualities, and exercised no powers, that men may not have through faith in Him. His perfect humanity is that which all His followers may possess, if they will be in subjection to God as He was.[530]

524–*Steps to Christ*, p. 89.
525–*The Review and Herald*, November 27, 1900.
526–*The Signs of the Times*, February 24, 1909.
527–*Testimonies to Ministers and Gospel Workers*, p. 113.
528–*Steps to Christ*, p. 88.
529–*The Review and Herald*, January 25, 1898.
530–*God's Amazing Grace*, p. 230.

Seeing Jesus

The reason that we carelessly indulge in sin is that we do not see Jesus. We would not lightly regard sin, did we appreciate the fact that sin wounds our Lord. Did we know Jesus by an experimental knowledge, we would not esteem duty as of small importance; but would manifest faithful integrity in the performance of every service. A right estimate of the character of God would enable us rightly to represent Him to the world. Harshness, roughness in words or manner, evilspeaking, passionate words, cannot exist in the soul that is looking unto Jesus. He who abides in Christ is in an atmosphere that forbids evil, and gives not the slightest excuse for anything of this kind.[531]

It is a law both of the intellectual and the spiritual nature that by beholding we become changed. The mind gradually adapts itself to the subjects upon which it is allowed to dwell. It becomes assimilated to that which it is accustomed to love and reverence.[532] Keep your eyes fixed on His perfection, and you walk in the light of Heaven. Through the power of the manifestation of divine glory, you constantly increase in spiritual understanding.[533] The divine illumination will increase more and more, corresponding with our onward movements, qualifying us to meet the responsibilities and emergencies before us.[534]

The more you know of the life, teachings, and character of Jesus, the more you will love Him. The better you understand the self-denial and self-sacrifice of Christ in behalf of fallen man, the more in earnest you will be to identify yourself and all your interests with Jesus Christ.[535]

Christian Unity

God's Word sets forth the will that is to be carried into the recesses of the soul. If the human agent consents, God can and will so identify His will with all our thoughts and aims, so blend our hearts and minds into conformity to His Word, that when obeying His will we are only carrying out the impulses of our minds. All such will not possess an unsanctified, selfish disposition, ready to carry out their own wills, but will have a jealous, earnest, determined zeal for the glory of God. They will not want to do anything in their own strength, and will guard strictly against the danger of promoting self.

All who would perfect a Christian character must wear the yoke of Christ. If they would sit together in heavenly places in Christ Jesus, they must learn of Him while on this Earth. Our natures are in need of discipline. They must be conformed to the nature of Jesus Christ, that He may accomplish the good He designs to do for all who will submit to be molded by yielding their natures to His authority. The great Teacher will yoke up with every soul who will bear His yoke.[536]

The very first work we are to do is to unite in the bonds of Christian fellowship. Those who are working for God should put away all unkind criticism, and

---

531–*The Youth's Instructor*, February 10, 1898.
532–*The Great Controversy*, p. 555.
533–*The Signs of the Times*, March 26, 1902.
534–*Testimonies for the Church*, vol. 3, p. 542.
535–*The Youth's Instructor*, August 18, 1886.
536–*Manuscript Releases*, vol. 10, p. 295.

draw together in unity. Christ desires His soldiers to stand shoulder to shoulder, united in the work of fighting the battles of the cross. He desires the union between those who work for Him to be as close as the union between Him and His Father. Those who have felt the sanctifying power of the Holy Spirit will heed the lessons of the divine Instructor, and will show their sincerity by doing all in their power to work in harmony with their brethren.[537]

There is to be unity in diversity. Every one is to be earnest in endeavoring to keep the unity of the Spirit in the bonds of peace. One man's thought is not to control, but minds are to be united under the great Head, as the branches are united to the vine. Believers in the Saviour Who gave His life for them, they are to work together in harmony. There will be no friction, for they will realize that they are called to the belief and knowledge of the truth as it is in Jesus. Those who are partakers of the divine nature will be one in spirit with Christ. "For he that is joined unto the Lord is one spirit" (1 Corinthians 6:17).[538]

Love One Another

Especially should those who have tasted the love of Christ develop their social powers, for in this way they may win souls to the Saviour. Christ should not be hid away in their hearts, shut in as a coveted treasure, sacred and sweet, to be enjoyed solely by themselves; nor should the love of Christ be manifested toward those only who please their fancy. Students are to be taught the Christlikeness of exhibiting a kindly interest, a social disposition, toward those who are in the greatest need, even though these may not be their own chosen companions. At all times and in all places Jesus manifested a loving interest in the human family and shed about Him the light of a cheerful piety.[539]

In [Christ's] first disciples was presented marked diversity. They were to be the world's teachers, and they represented widely varied types of character. In order successfully to carry forward the work to which they had been called, these men, differing in natural characteristics and in habits of life, needed to come into unity of feeling, thought, and action. This unity it was Christ's object to secure. To this end He sought to bring them into unity with Himself.[540]

"As Thou hast sent Me into the world, even so have I also sent them into the world. And for their sakes I sanctify Myself, that they also might be sanctified through the truth. Neither pray I for these alone, but for them also which shall believe on Me through their Word; that they all may be one, as Thou, Father, art in Me and I in Thee, that they also may be one in Us; that the world may believe that Thou hast sent Me." [John 17:18–21.] These words present the grand result of Christian unity. Christians are to be one in Christ. By their unity they are to bear witness to the world that Christ is the Sent of God. All true disciples will realize that this is the standard they must reach. They will strive continually to help one another.[541]

537–*The Review and Herald*, October 29, 1901.
538–*Manuscript Releases*, vol. 11, pp. 178, 179.
539–*The Adventist Home*, pp. 457, 458.
540–*The Acts of the Apostles*, p. 20.
541–*The Signs of the Times*, June 19, 1901.

God With Us

Here, where the Son of God tabernacled in humanity; where the King of glory lived and suffered and died, —here, when He shall make all things new, the tabernacle of God shall be with men, "and He shall dwell with them, and they shall be His people, and God Himself, shall be with them, and be their God." [Revelation 21:3.] And through endless ages as the redeemed walk in the light of the Lord, they will praise Him for His unspeakable Gift, Immanuel, "God with us." [Matthew 1:23.][542]

---

[542]–*The Review and Herald*, February 25, 1915.

Bibliography

This bibliography contains the sources that were used in this book, which were all authored by Ellen G. White. The list is separated into two sections—books and periodicals.

Books

The Acts of the Apostles. Mountain View, CA: Pacific Press Publishing Association, 1911.

The Adventist Home. Hagerstown, MD: Review and Herald Publishing Association, 1952.

An Appeal to the Youth. Battle Creek, MI: Seventh-day Adventist Publishing Association, 1864.

Child Guidance. Washington, DC: Review and Herald Publishing Association, 1954.

Christ Triumphant. Hagerstown, MD: Review and Herald Publishing Association, 1999.

Christian Experience and Teachings of Ellen G. White. Mountain View, CA: Pacific Press Publishing Association, 1922.

Christ's Object Lessons. Washington, DC: Review and Herald Publishing Association, 1900.

Colporteur Ministry. Mountain View, CA: Pacific Press Publishing Association, 1953.

Counsels on Health. Mountain View, CA: Pacific Press Publishing Association, 1923.

Counsels on Sabbath School Work. Washington, DC: Review and Herald Publishing Association, 1938.

The Desire of Age. Mountain View, CA: Pacific Press Publishing Association, 1898.

Early Writings. Washington, DC: Review and Herald Publishing Association, 1882.

Education. Mountain View, CA: Pacific Press Publishing Association, 1903.

The Ellen G. White 1888 Materials. Washington, DC: Ellen G. White Estate, 1987.

Evangelism. Washington, DC: Review and Herald Publishing Association, 1946.

The Faith I Live By. Washington, DC: Review and Herald Publishing Association, 1958.

God's Amazing Grace. Washington, DC: Review and Herald Publishing Association, 1973.

Gospel Workers. Washington, DC: Review and Herald Publishing Association, 1915.

The Great Controversy. Mountain View, CA: Pacific Press Publishing Association, 1911.

Historical Sketches of the Foreign Missions of the Seventh-day Adventists. Basle: Imprimerie Polyglotte, 1886.

In Heavenly Places. Washington, DC: Review and Herald Publishing Association, 1967.

Manuscript Releases. Vol. 3. Silver Spring, MD: Ellen G. White Estate, 1990.

Manuscript Releases. Vol. 6. Silver Spring, MD: Ellen G. White Estate, 1990.

Manuscript Releases. Vol. 10. Silver Spring, MD: Ellen G. White Estate, 1990.

Manuscript Releases. Vol. 11. Silver Spring, MD: Ellen G. White Estate, 1990.

Manuscript Releases. Vol. 13. Silver Spring, MD: Ellen G. White Estate, 1990.

Manuscript Releases. Vol. 20. Silver Spring, MD: Ellen G. White Estate, 1993.

Manuscript Releases. Vol. 21. Silver Spring, MD: Ellen G. White Estate, 1993.

Maranatha. Washginton, DC: Review and Herald Publishing Association, 1976.

Medical Ministry. Mountain View, CA: Pacific Press Publishing Association, 1932.

Messages to Young People. Hagerstown, MD: Review and Herald Publishing Association, 1930.

Mind, Character, and Personality. Vol. 1. Nashville, TN: Southern Publishing Association, 1977.

The Ministry of Healing. Mountain View, CA: Pacific Press Publishing Association, 1905.

My Life Today. Washington, DC: Review and Herald Publishing Associaiton, 1952.

Our High Calling. Washington, DC: Review and Herald Publishing Association, 1961.

Patriarchs and Prophets. Washington, DC: Review and Herald Publishing Association, 1890.

Prophets and Kings. Mountain View, CA: Pacific Press Publishing Association, 1917.

Reflecting Christ. Hagerstown, MD: Review and Herald Publishing Association, 1985.

Selected Messages. Book 1. Washington, DC: Review and Herald Publishing Association, 1958.

Selected Messages. Book 2. Washington, DC: Review and Herald Publishing Association, 1958.

Selected Messages. Book 3. Washington, DC: Review and Herald Publishing Association, 1980.

Sons and Daughters of God. Washington, DC: Review and Herald Publishing Association, 1955.

Spalding and Magan Collection. Payson, AZ: Leaves-Of-Autumn Books, 1985.

Special Testimonies on Education. No imprint, 1897.

The Spirit of Prophecy. Vol. 1. Battle Creek, MI: Seventh-day Adventist Publishing Association, 1870.

The Spirit of Prophecy. Vol. 4. Battle Creek, MI: Seventh-day Adventist Publishing Association, 1884.

Spiritual Gifts. Vol. 2. Battle Creek, MI: Seventh-day Adventist Publishing Association, 1860.

Steps to Christ. Mountain View, CA: Pacific Press Publishing Association, 1892.

Temperance. Mountain View, CA: Pacific Press Publishing Association, 1949.

Testimonies for the Church. Vol. 1. Mountain View, CA: Pacific Press Publishing Association, 1868.

Testimonies for the Church. Vol. 2. Mountain View, CA: Pacific Press Publishing Association, 1871.

Testimonies for the Church. Vol. 3. Mountain View, CA: Pacific Press Publishing Association, 1875.

Testimonies for the Church. Vol. 4. Mountain View, CA: Pacific Press Publishing Association, 1881.

Testimonies for the Church. Vol. 5. Mountain View, CA: Pacific Press Publishing Association, 1889.

Testimonies for the Church. Vol. 6. Mountain View, CA: Pacific Press Publishing Association, 1901.

Testimonies for the Church. Vol. 7. Mountain View, CA: Pacific Press Publishing Association, 1902.

Testimonies for the Church. Vol. 8. Mountain View, CA: Pacific Press Publishing Association, 1904.

Testimonies for the Church. Vol. 9. Mountain View, CA: Pacific Press Publishing Association, 1909.

Testimonies to Ministers and Gospel Workers. Mountain View, CA: Pacific Press Publishing Association, 1923.

That I May Know Him. Washington, DC: Review and Herald Publishing Association, 1964.

This Day With God. Washington, DC: Review and Herald Publishing Association, 1979.

Thoughts from the Mount of Blessing. Mountain View, CA: Pacific Press Publishing Association, 1896.

The Upward Look. Washington, DC: Review and Herald Publishing Association, 1982.

Welfare Ministry. Washington, DC: Review and Herald Publishing Association, 1952.

Periodicals

"Abiding in Christ." *The Signs of the Times,* June 8, 1891.

"The Abiding Rest." *The Signs of the Times,* July 6, 1904.

"Acceptable Prayer." *The Review and Herald,* May 28, 1895.

"Address and Appeal, Setting Forth the Importance of Missionary Work." *The Review and Herald,* January 2, 1879.

"An All-Powerful Saviour." *The Youth's Instructor,* September 21, 1899.

"Are We Growing Up Into Christ?" *The Bible Echo,* April 15, 1892.

"At Simon's House." *The Signs of the Times,* May 9, 1900.

"Be Watchful." *The Review and Herald,* July 7, 1910.

"Bible Religion." *The Signs of the Times,* February 24, 1890.

"Brotherly Love." *The Signs of the Times,* February 1, 1883.

"Brotherly Love Needed." *The Review and Herald,* October 24, 1893.

"Business Principles of the Christian." *The Signs of the Times,* February 24, 1909.

"By Their Fruits Ye Shall Know Them." *The Signs of the Times,* July 11, 1892.

"Camp-Meetings." *General Conference Daily Bulletin,* March 2, 1899.

"The Character of the Law of God." *The Signs of the Times,* April 15, 1886.
"Christ as Teacher." *The Review and Herald,* November 28, 1893.
"Christian Courtesy." *The Review and Herald,* September 1, 1885.
"The Christian's Privilege." *The Review and Herald,* May 3, 1881.
"Christlike Religion." *The Youth's Instructor,* February 17, 1898.
"Christ's Followers the Light of the World." *The Review and Herald,* May 13, 1884.
"Christ's Instruction to His Followers." *The Review and Herald,* April 26, 1892.
"Christ's Prayer for Us." *The Signs of the Times,* June 19, 1901.
"Christ's Righteousness Avails." *The Bible Echo,* April 1, 1893.
"The Church Must Be Quickened." *The Review and Herald,* January 17, 1893.
"The Church's Great Need." *The Review and Herald,* March 22, 1887.
"Come Ye Yourselves Apart, ... and Rest Awhile." *The Review and Herald,* November 7, 1893.
"Conditions of Prevailing Prayer." *The Signs of the Times,* August 21, 1884.
"Connection With Christ." *The Review and Herald,* November 23, 1897.
"Consecration and Diligence in Christian Workers." *The Review and Herald,* June 24, 1884.
"Courage in the Lord." *The Review and Herald,* May 5, 1910.
"The Crucifixion of Self." *The Signs of the Times,* April 9, 1902.
"The Danger of Talking Doubt." *The Review and Herald,* February 11, 1890.
"Dangers of the Young." *The Review and Herald*, March 11, 1880.
"The Duty of Confession." *The Review and Herald,* December 16, 1890.
"The Duty of Forgiveness." *The Review and Herald,* November 16, 1886.
"Effectual Prayer." *The Review and Herald,* April 22, 1884.
"Faith and Good Works." *The Signs of the Times,* May 19, 1898.
"Faith and Works." *The Signs of the Times,* March 30, 1888.
"Faithfulness in Health Reform." *The Review and Herald,* March 3, 1910.

"Faithfulness in Little Things." *The Youth's Instructor,* January 28, 1897.

"For a Witness Unto All Nations." *The Review and Herald,* November 14, 1912.

"The Fruit of True Faith." *The Youth's Instructor,* February 10, 1898.

General Conference Bulletin, October 1, 1896.

"Go, Preach the Gospel." *The Youth's Instructor,* June 24, 1897.

"God's Care for His Church." *The Signs of the Times,* February 14, 1900.

"God's Object in Blessing His People." *The Signs of the Times,* February 10, 1890.

"God's Promises Our Plea." *The Southern Watchman,* June 4, 1903.

"God's Representatives." *The Youth's Instructor,* March 4, 1897.

"A Habitation for the Spirit." *The Review and Herald,* December 31, 1908.

"Heaven's Unspeakable Gift." *The Review and Herald,* February 25, 1915.

"In the Race for Eternal Life." *The Signs of the Times,* March 19, 1902.

"In Union With Christ." *The Review and Herald,* May 30, 1907.

"In What Shall We Glory?" *The Review and Herald,* March 15, 1887.

"Individual Consecration Needed." *The Review and Herald,* November 23, 1905.

"Judge Not." *The Signs of the Times,* March 14, 1892.

"Judge Not." *The Signs of the Times,* March 21, 1892.

"Judge Not." *The Review and Herald,* November 14, 1907.

"Judge Not–No. 1." *The Review and Herald,* October 29, 1901.

"Judge Not, That Ye Be Not Judged." *The Review and Herald,* August 16, 1892.

"Justification by Faith." *The Signs of the Times,* November 10, 1890.

"Keeping the Heart." *The Youth's Instructor,* March 5, 1903.

"Let Both Grow Together." *The Review and Herald,* January 3, 1893.

"Let Us Go Without the Camp." *The Review and Herald,* May 28, 1889.

"A Letter to a Church-Elder." *Atlantic Union Gleaner,* September 9, 1903.

Letter 22, 1901.

Letter 47, 1893.
Letter 88, 1906.
Letter 139, 1898.
"Life of Christ—No. 1." *The Youth's Instructor,* March 1, 1872.
"The Life of the New Man." *The Signs of the Times,* January 2, 1907.
"Look and Live." *The Signs of the Times,* March 10, 1890.
"Look Not to Self but to Christ." *The Signs of the Times,* April 9, 1894.
"The Lord's Prayer." *The Signs of the Times,* October 28, 1903.
"Love to God and Man." *The Signs of the Times,* August 3, 1876.
"Love Toward God and Man." *The Review and Herald,* September 20, 1906.
"Make Straight Paths for Your Feet." *The Review and Herald,* August 24, 1897.
"The Mirror." *The Youth's Instructor,* August 18, 1886.
"The Need of Earnest Labor for Others." *The Review and Herald,* April 29, 1909.
"The Need of Love." *The Review and Herald,* August 28, 1888.
"The New Year." *The Review and Herald,* December 16, 1884.
"Notes of Travel." *The Review and Herald,* November 4, 1884.
"Obedience and Its Reward." *The Signs of the Times,* September 15, 1887.
"Ordained to Bring Forth Fruit." *The Review and Herald,* February 12, 1895.
"Our Eternal Destiny Decided by Our Course Here." *The Signs of the Times,* July 31, 1893.
"Our Great Treasure-House." *The Signs of the Times,* September 12, 1906.
"Our Preparation for the End." *The Signs of the Times,* November 22, 1905.
"Our Words." *The Review and Herald,* February 16, 1897.
"Our Words–No. 2." *The Review and Herald,* January 25, 1898.
"Partakers of the Divine Nature." *The Review and Herald,* March 1, 1887.
"A Perfect Law." *The Signs of the Times,* July 31, 1901.
"The Power of Faith." *The Signs of the Times,* January 20, 1904.
"Pray for the Latter Rain." *The Review and Herald,* March 2, 1897.
"Pray Without Ceasing." *The Signs of the Times,* December 23, 1889.
"Prayer." *The Signs of the Times,* June 18, 1902.

"Prayer Our Stronghold." *The Youth's Instructor,* August 18, 1898.

"The Prayer That God Accepts." *The Review and Herald,* February 9, 1897.

"The Prayer That God Approves." *The Signs of the Times,* December 3, 1896.

"Prepare to Meet the Lord." *The Review and Herald,* November 27, 1900.

"The Privilege of Prayer." *The Review and Herald,* December 8, 1904.

"The Promise of the Spirit." *The Review and Herald,* April 30, 1908.

"Remarks by Mrs. E. G. White." *General Conference Bulletin,* April 5, 1901.

"The Renewing of the Mind." *The Review and Herald,* June 12, 1888.

"The Results of Abiding in Christ." *Sabbath-School Worker,* July 1, 1894.

"The Science of Salvation the First of Sciences." *The Review and Herald,* December 1, 1891.

"Sin Condemned in the Flesh." *The Signs of the Times,* January 16, 1896.

"The Spirit of a Christian." *The Review and Herald,* February 24, 1891.

"Striking Examples of Prayer." *The Signs of the Times,* August 14, 1884.

"A Teacher Sent From God." *The Signs of the Times,* June 7, 1905.

"Tempted in All Points Like as We Are." *The Bible Echo,* November 1, 1892.

"A Time for Prevailing Prayer." *The Review and Herald,* December 14, 1905.

"The Truth Revealed in Jesus." *The Review and Herald,* February 8, 1898.

"The Two Covenants." *The Review and Herald,* October 17, 1907.

"The Value of Prayer." *The Signs of the Times,* November 18, 1886.

"The Vine and the Branches–2." *The Review and Herald,* November 9, 1897.

"Words of Greeting From Sister White [to the General Conference]." *The Review and Herald,* May 29, 1913.

"Words to Christians." *The Signs of the Times,* March 26, 1902.
"Words to the Young." *The Youth's Instructor,* June 1, 1893.
"Words to the Young." *The Youth's Instructor,* February 8, 1894.
"Words to the Young." *The Youth's Instructor,* June 7, 1894.
"Words to the Young." *The Youth's Instructor,* September 13, 1894.
"The Work Before Us." *The Review and Herald,* July 1, 1909.
"Working as Christ Worked." *Pacific Health Journal,* December 1, 1901.
"Ye Are Complete in Him." *The Bible Echo,* January 15, 1892.
"Ye Are Not Your Own." *The Bible Echo,* October 15, 1900.

We invite you to view the complete
selection of titles we publish at:

www.TEACHServices.com

scan with your mobile
device to go directly
to our website

Please write or email us your praises, reactions, or
thoughts about this or any other book we publish at:

P.O. Box 954
Ringgold, GA 30736

Info@TEACHServices.com

TEACH Services, Inc., titles may be purchased in bulk for
educational, business, fund-raising, or sales promotional use.
For information, please e-mail:

BulkSales@TEACHServices.com

Finally if you are interested in seeing
your own book in print, please contact us at

publishing@TEACHServices.com

We would be happy to review your manuscript for free.

www.ingramcontent.com/pod-product-compliance
Lightning Source LLC
Chambersburg PA
CBHW081924170426
43200CB00014B/2826